Watercolor Jacket

by Diana Leone

Leone Publications

Mountain View, California

ISBN 0-942786-37-8

Leone Publications

264 Castro Street, Mountain View, California 94041 U.S.A.

(415) 965-9797   Fax (415) 965-9799

Watercolor Jacket

Contents

Check off each step as you complete it.

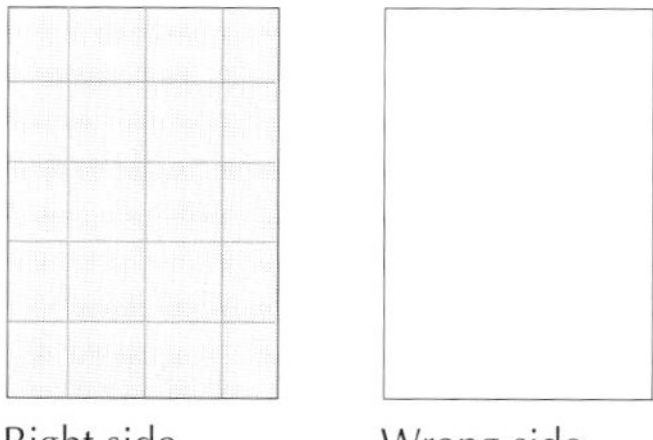
Right side   Wrong side

Diana's Watercolor Jacket

General Instructions

Read all instructions before cutting or sewing.

Make a "watercolor" or "impressionist" jacket by arranging 2" by 2" squares of fabric from dark at the bottom row to light at the top, using Diana's value of color lesson, on page 7.

Seam Allowances

Use a ¼" seam allowance when sewing the 2" squares together.

Unless otherwise noted, use a ½" seam allowance throughout the jacket construction. The seam allowance is included in the jacket pattern and the assembly directions.

The Squares

The squares are cut 2" by 2". The finished, sewn squares are 1½" by 1½".

Use **both** sides of the 2" fabric squares. The inside of the fabric is usually a much lighter value and can be used as a light value.

You need approximately 1,200 to 1,500 2" squares. 1 yard of fabric is enough for about 360 2" squares; 3½ yards of fabric will yield almost 1,500 2" squares. You will not use all of the squares, but you need the selection to create your jacket.

Modifying the Pattern

This pattern is multi-sized and includes petite through extra large. You may adapt the pattern fit to your individual requirements. Shorten or lengthen the sleeve and jacket pattern pieces before cutting the pieced fabric panels. For a looser fit, leave the elastic out of the bottom edge.

Shoulder pads are optional. Make fabric-covered shoulder pads and sew them inside the jacket shoulder seam before attaching the lining.

In the illustrations, the right side of the fabric is indicated by a gray grid; solid white indicates the wrong side of the fabric.

Supplies & Materials

Fabric Requirements

Outer Fabric: 4½ yds. of 100% cotton, divided as follows:

¼ yd. of 20 different prints (florals, textures, or any style print) light to dark; or

⅜ yd. of 10 to 15 different fabrics, light to dark

Front Band and Pocket Fabric:

½ yd. of 100% cotton, if a different fabric than the lining fabric

Lining Fabric:

(includes front band, pocket and jacket body lining)

3½ yds. 42" wide 100% cotton, polyester-cotton blend, polyester or silk lining

Creative Grid©* 4 yds. of 42" wide, 100% cotton gridded or white flannel: Use this flannel as a design area to lay out the 2" squares

Batting: 4 yds. white flannel

Note: The design wall flannel (Creative Grid©) can be used for the batting.

**See buyer's guide on page 32.*

All supplies can be ordered directly from The Quilting Bee, 357 Castro Street, Mountain View, CA 94041.

Notions

The following notions are used to assemble the jacket. You may already have some of these tools in your sewing supply. Use an item similar to the one listed if it will work, before you purchase any of the notions listed.

★ **¼" foot** for machine piecing the squares

★ **"Walking foot",** "Even Feed", or "Dual feed" for straight line machine quilting

★ **Darning foot** or free-motion foot for free-motion machine quilting

★ **Sewing machine needles:**

Machine needle: "Jeans" or a new sharp needle, size 12 or 14 for all piecing

"Metafil" or "top stitch 140-N" size 14 or 16, to use with rayon and metallic threads for machine quilting

★ **Threads:**

100% Cotton thread: large spool of a neutral color for piecing (Mettler is an excellent brand)

Clear or dark YLI™ or Sulky® monofilament thread (size .004), Mettler®, Madeira®, and Sulky® are good metallic threads to use in the bobbin or top for machine quilting

★ **Safety pins:**

300 size 0 brass safety pins for basting the 3 layers together before machine quilting

One size 3 safety pin for pulling elastic through sleeve casing

• **Pattern tracing material:** medium weight interfacing, pattern paper or tracing paper for tracing the pattern

• **Mild soap:** Orvus "Quilt soap"

• **Straight Pins:** 500 small, thin "Tru-Point™" or fine pins

• **Buttons:** Six or seven, ⅞"

★ **Elastic**: 2 yds. ¾" or 1" for waistband and sleeves

• **Rotary cutter, mat and cutting guide**

• **Scissors**

★ **Sewing Machine** in great working order

★ Important to have

• Substitutions may be used

Selecting the Fabrics

A variety of textures, prints, florals, and geometrics may be combined to make your jacket. Why not use all plaids, or all black with white and gray prints? For a colorwash look, use all florals, or florals mixed with textures.

Prints with a low contrast may be the easiest to use. These are monotones, or print on print. Floral prints with a lot of contrast in the background will also work. Prints with high contrast may be more difficult to use, but any fabric will work. Don't be afraid to experiment.

To create the colorwash or impressionist look, use small, blended prints that are similar in value. The subtle changes in value make these fabrics blend easily from one to the next.

Select as many fabrics as you like. Twenty is better than ten; thirty is better than twenty. A full range of print style and value (from light to dark) will be helpful in creating your impressionistic jacket. It may be hard to find light values; use the wrong side of the fabrics to add variety in value.

Some of the fabrics may not work into your final design. It's okay not to use all of the squares that you cut. Save your squares for another project, or make another jacket for a friend.

Preparing the Fabrics

For a soft, antiqued look, do not shrink the fabric for the outer jacket or the flannel batting before it is cut and assembled.

The pattern allows for the shrinkage of the jacket. If you do not want an antiqued look, pre-shrink all of the fabrics before cutting the squares. Antiquing is described on page 16.

Pre-shrink the cotton lining fabric before cutting and assembly.

Cutting the 2" Squares

Use a rotary cutter, mat, and cutting guide to cut the outer jacket fabrics into 2" squares. The edge of the cut fabric is your sewing guide. Cutting and sewing accuracy is very important. Make sure the squares are exactly 2" on all sides.

If you don't have a rotary cutter, use very sharp scissors. I recommend Gingher® 7".

Cut all of the outer jacket fabrics into 2" squares. Don't count how many squares there are—just get started!

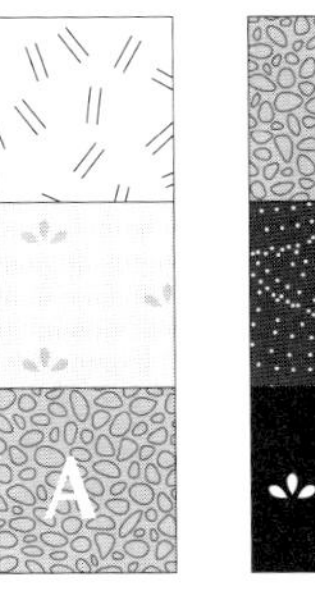

The Value of Color

Value is the relationship of light to dark. Value is relative—a medium fabric (see A at left) may be a dark in a light group and may appear to be a light in a dark group. Learning to see the value of a fabric will help you to determine its placement, and create a pleasing blend of hues.

Use the Value Chart to practice seeing the value of the fabrics. Find the gray value similar to the value of your fabrics. Place each fabric square next to whichever value most closely matches the chart. For fabrics with more than one value (multi-value prints), place where they most closely match. The value of some fabrics may be very hard to determine; set these fabrics aside, and use them if you can.

Sort all of the fabric squares from dark to light and store them in a pizza box until you are ready to assemble them.

Value Chart

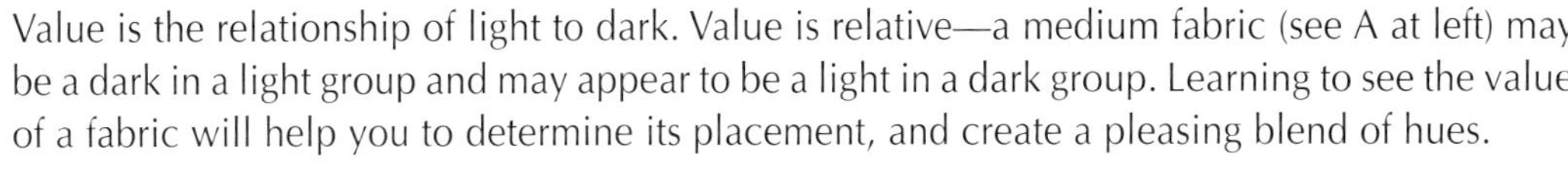

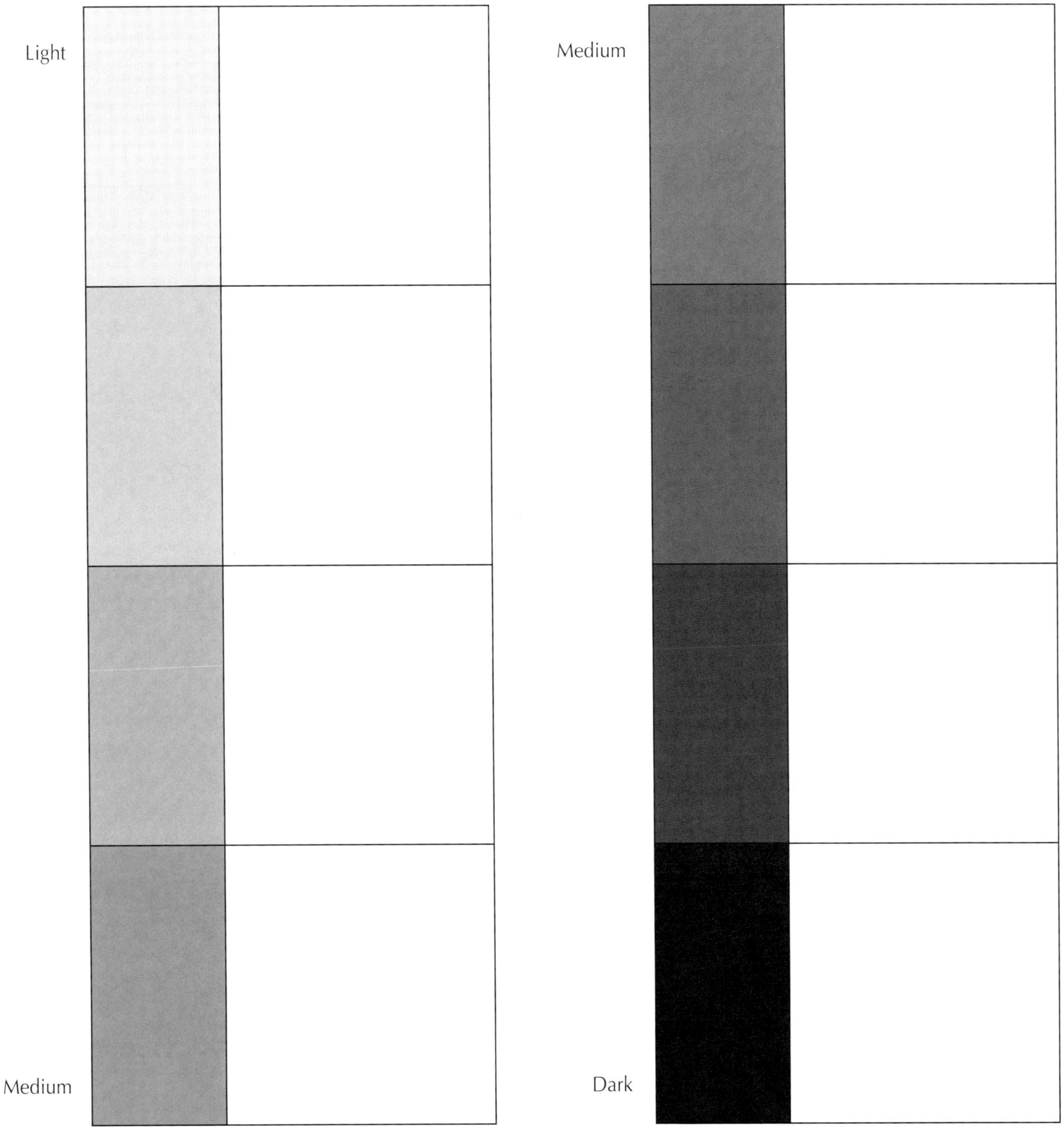

Light

Medium

Medium

Dark

Arranging the 2" Squares

The fabric squares can be arranged in any color or pattern design that appeals to you.

The jacket on the front cover is made of all light-colored pastel florals. The darkest values are at the bottom, and the lightest values at the top. Similar colors and values are grouped together to achieve a floral garden effect.

The teal jacket on the back cover is arranged from dark at the bottom to light at the top. The wrong side of many of the fabrics was used to add a variety of light values.

Assembling the Panels

The area needed for the layout of the jacket panels is 50% larger than the actual pieced panels, because the panels will be smaller after the squares are sewn together.

Build the panels on one continuous piece of flannel, as shown below.

Begin with the back panel. Starting with the bottom row, place the 2" squares onto the flannel. The bottom row is the guide for cutting the jacket parts. It is important to keep this row straight.

Place the squares on the flannel, beginning at the bottom of each panel. Place the squares however you wish in rows from the bottom up until the rectangles are formed. Refer to the layout diagrams on the opposite page for ideas.

To build the panels from light to dark, place the darkest fabrics along the bottom row. Place one of the lightest fabrics at the top. Build the panel from the darkest to the lightest.

Pin the squares to the flannel to make the panels needed to cut your jacket size. The two fronts, two sleeves, and collar are made in the same manner. You may piece the front bands, or you may use a single piece of fabric for each band.

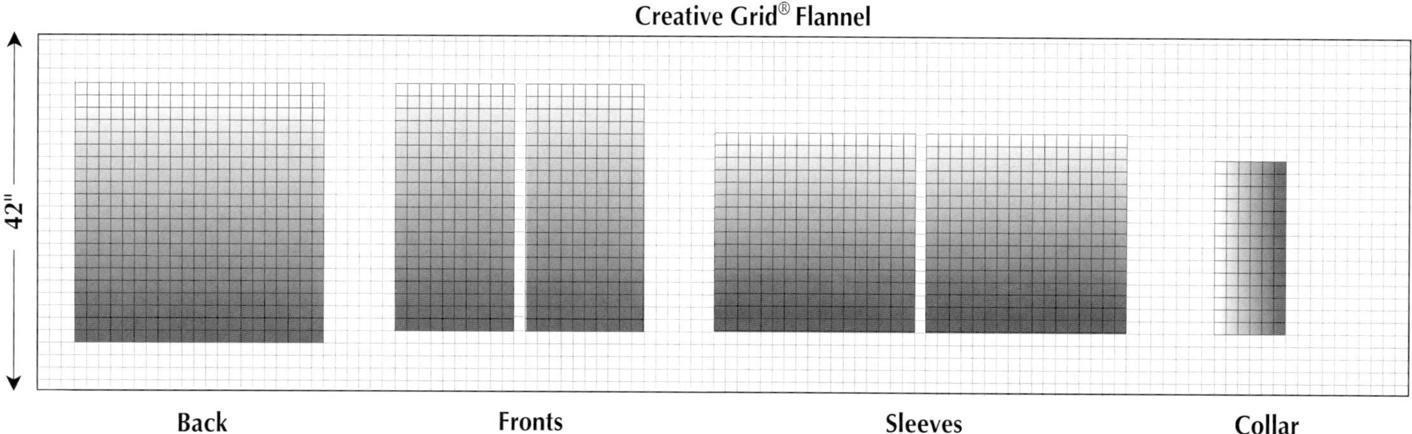

Layout Ideas

Use the value chart on page 7 to find the value of your fabrics.

Use these designs to create your own variations.

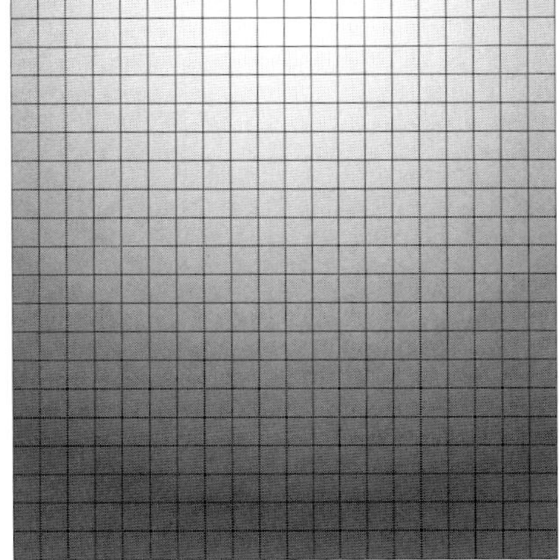

Dark at the bottom to light at the top.

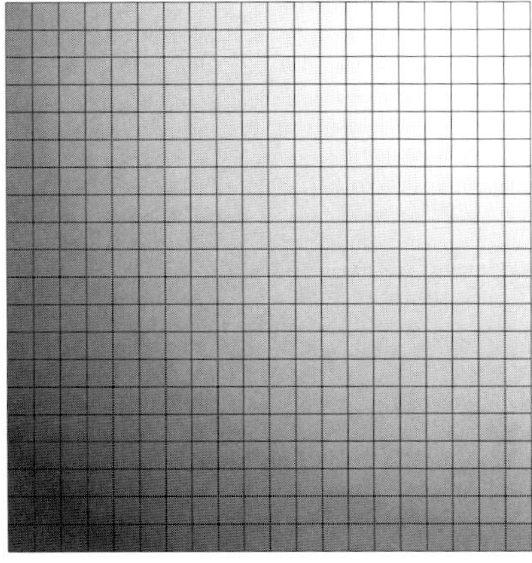

Dark at one corner to light at the opposite corner.

Diagonal dark to light strips.

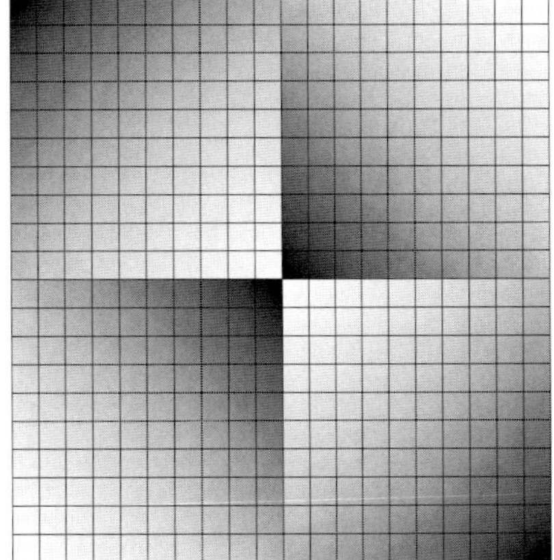

Dark and light centers.

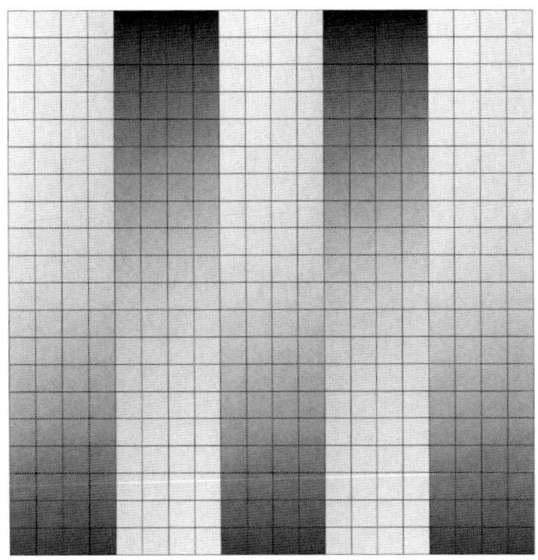

Dark and light alternating bands.

A square within a square.

Number of 2" Squares Needed to Build the Panels

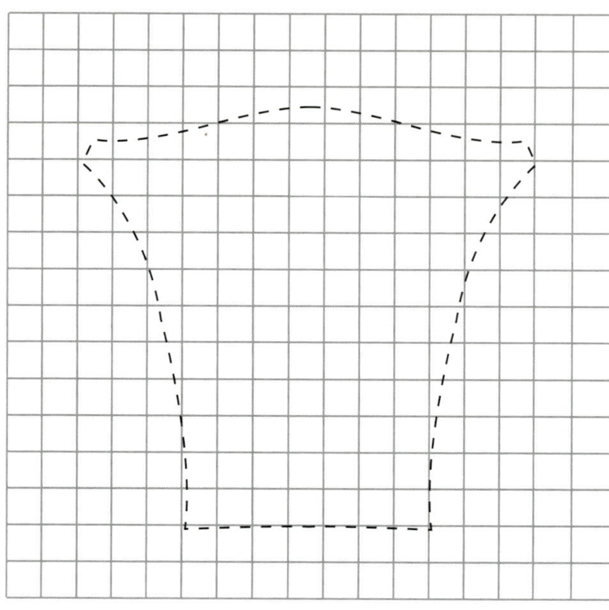

The flannel area needed to lay out the squares is 50% larger than the pieced sleeve.

One Collar

All Sizes   6

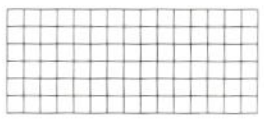

15 squares

One Back

Width

Height
18   20   21   24   24

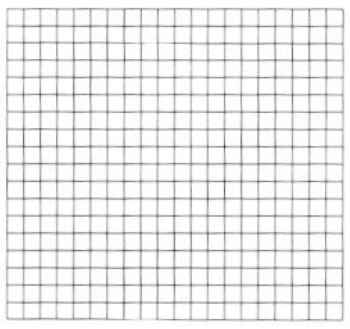

20 squares
Petite

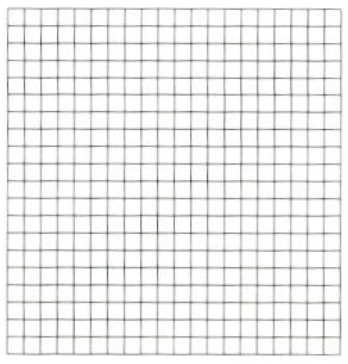

20 squares
Small

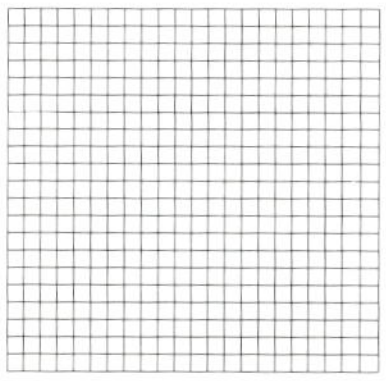

22 squares
Medium

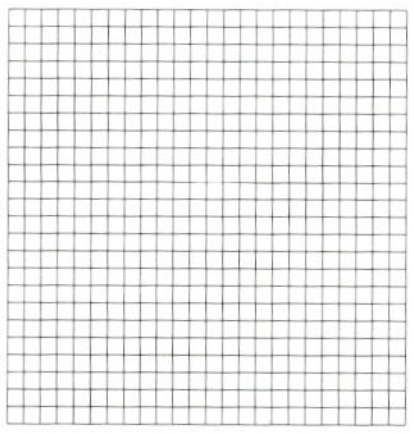

24 squares
Large

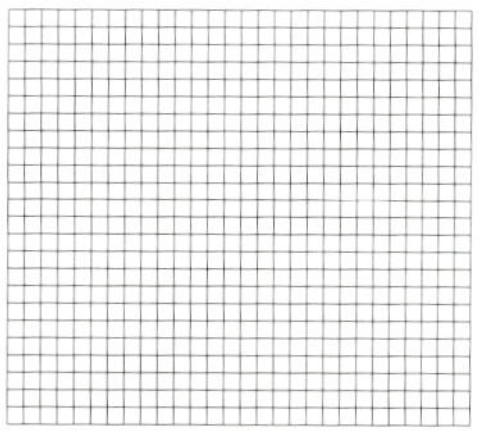

28 squares
Extra-Large

Two Fronts

19   20   21   24   24

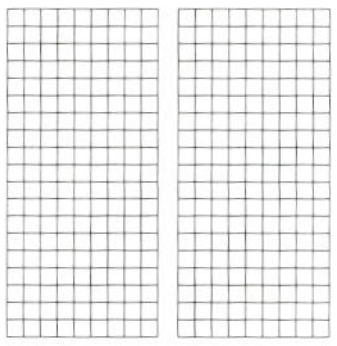

9 squares
Petite

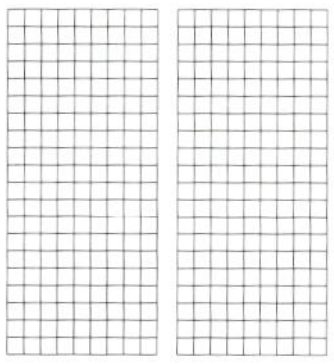

9 squares
Small

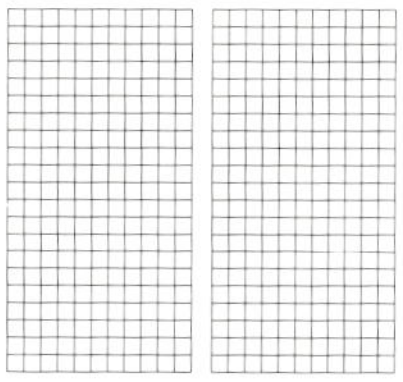

11 squares
Medium

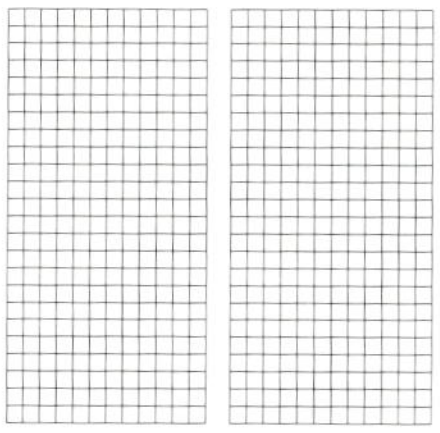

12 squares
Large

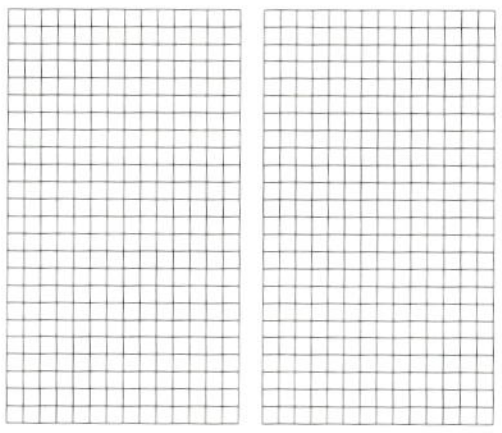

14 squares
Extra-Large

Two Sleeves

14   15   17   18

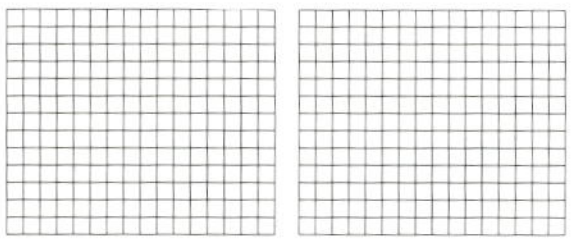

16 squares
Petite

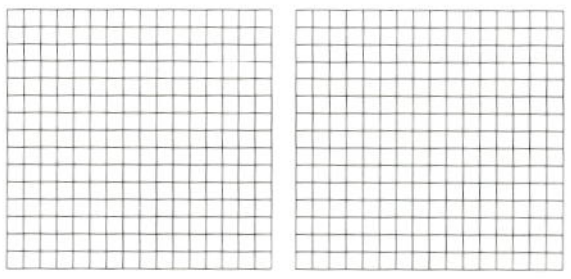

16 squares
Small

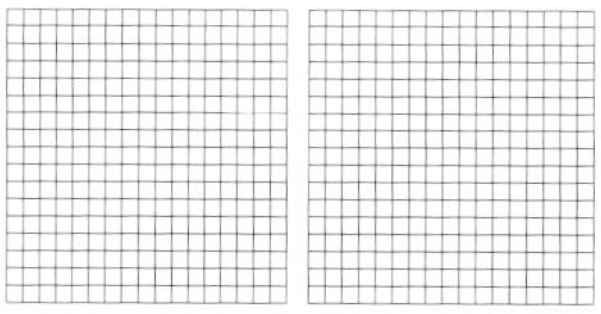

17 squares
Medium

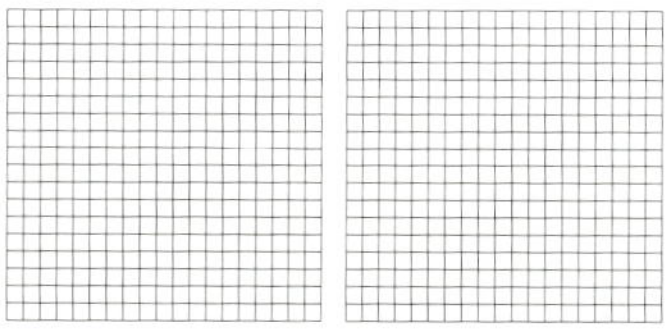

19 squares
Large / Extra Large

Piecing the Squares into Panels

Sew the 2" squares into one rectangle for the back, two rectangles for the fronts, two rectangles for the sleeves, and one for the collar.

Machine quilt the pieced back, front, sleeve, and collar panels to a single layer of cotton flannel.

Wash the fabric panels to antique them if you wish.

The jacket parts are cut from these panels.

Cut the front bands as two rectangles and machine quilt them with a single layer of flannel. Wash the bands. Re-cut the bands to the size needed to fit the front jacket length.

Assemble the jacket and lining.

Pieced panel.

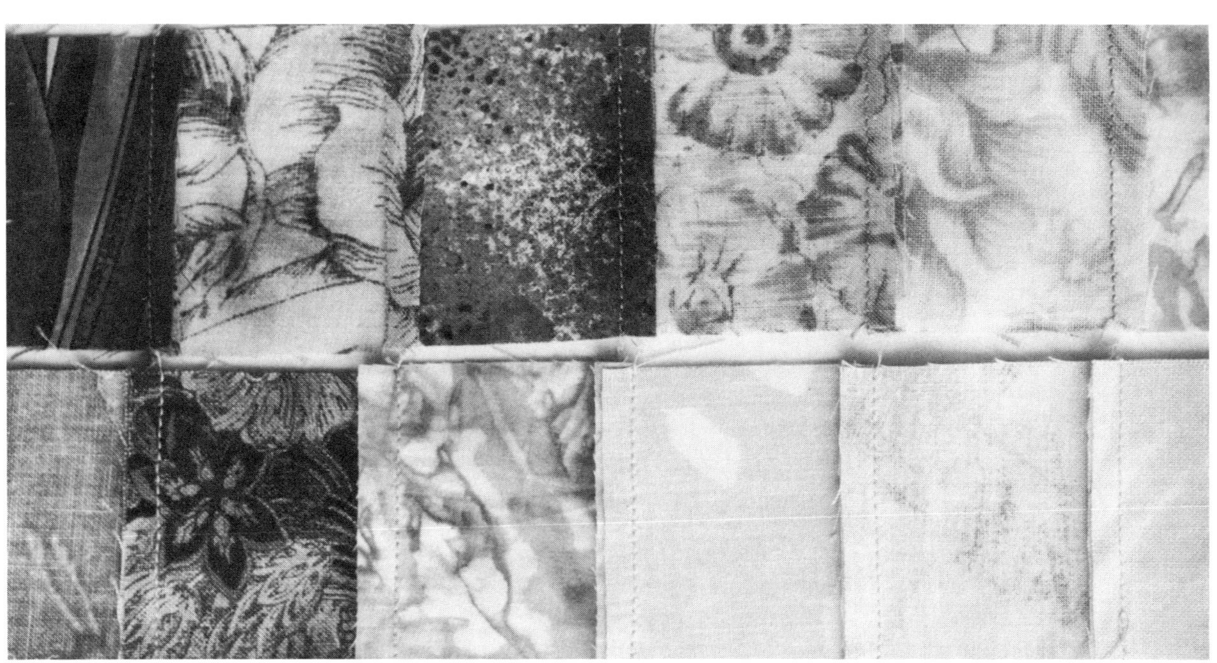

Sew the squares into rows, using a ¼" seam.

Press the seams of each row in one direction. Alternate the pressing direction for each row.

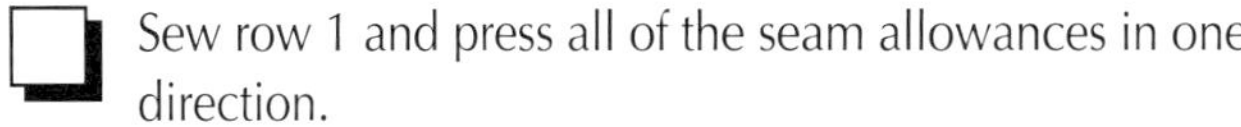

Sew row 1 and press all of the seam allowances in one direction.

Sew row 2 and press all of the seam allowances in the opposite direction.

Sew all of the rows together.

Pin and sew all of the pieced rows together.

Press all of the seams in one direction.

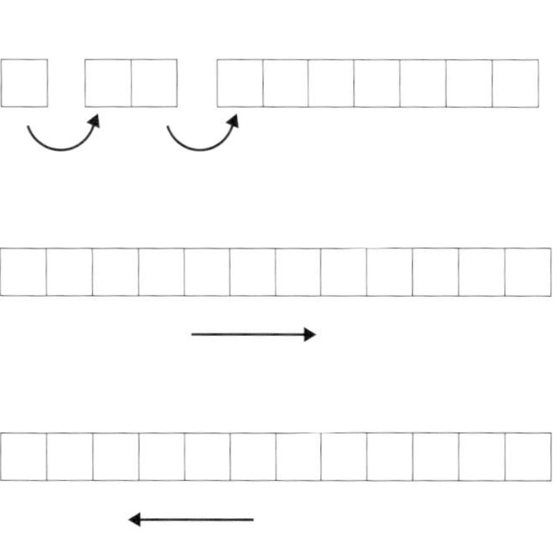

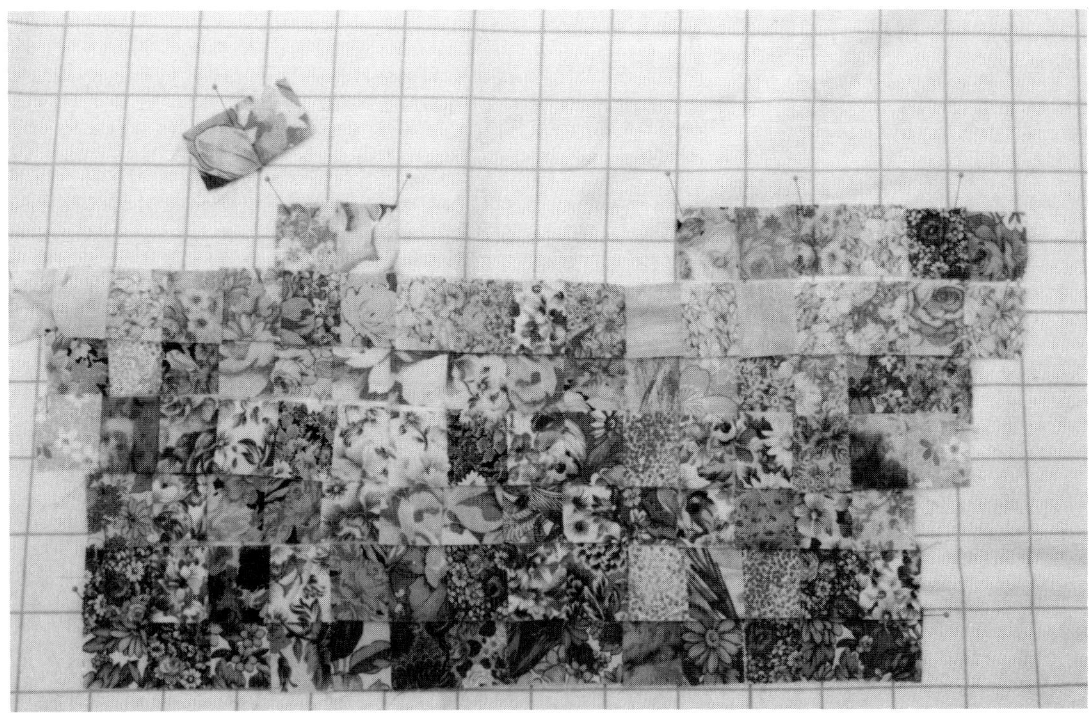

Back panel. The panels are worked from the bottom towards the top.
The rows are then sewn together.

A sewn back.

Pieced collar.

Pieced fronts.

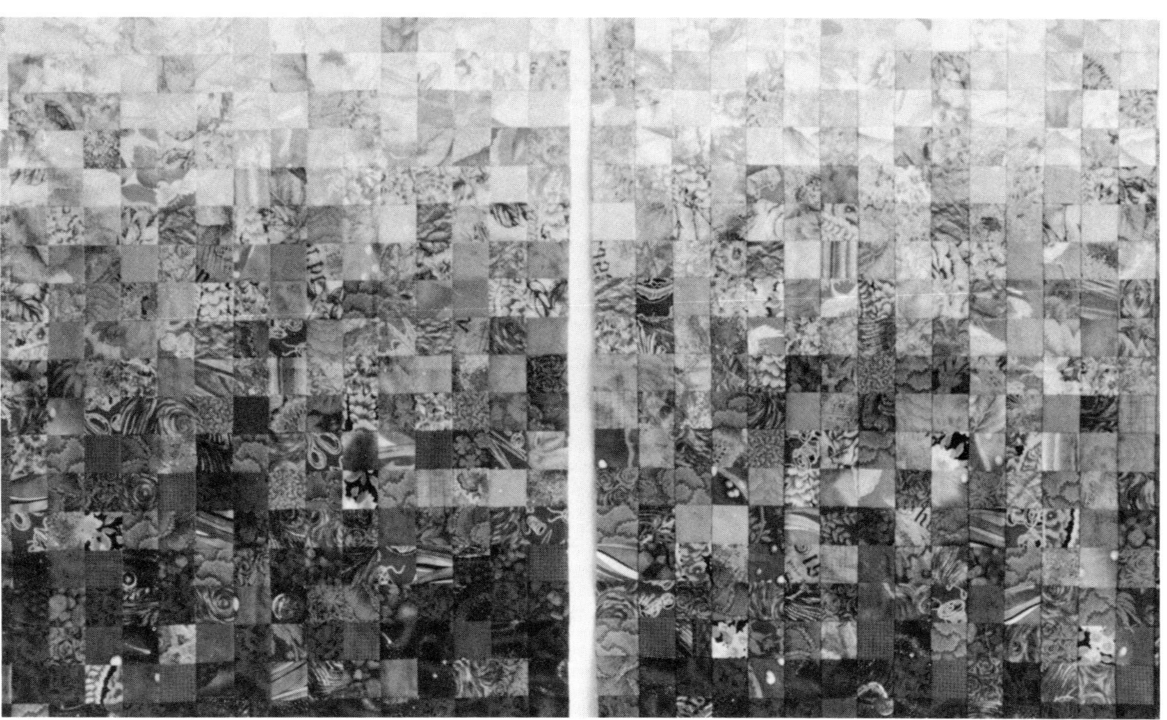

Pieced sleeves.

General Instructions for Machine Quilting

Before you begin, read through all of the directions for straight line and stipple quilting.

Your jacket can be quilted using either straight line or stipple quilting, or a combination of both.

Before beginning to quilt your jacket, practice on a sample after you have read the directions.

- Pin-baste the pieced fabric panels to the flannel batting. Use size 0 brass safety pins. Safety pin-baste every other square, or every 2" to 3", or use the "Quilter's Basting Gun"®.

- Use a sharp, new "Jeans" or "Denim" needle, size 12 or 14 for 100% cotton thread.

- Use a "Topstitch" or "Metafil" needle for metallic threads.

- Use clear thread, matching cotton thread, or a metallic thread on the top. Use a neutral cotton thread in the bobbin.

- It is not necessary to mark lines on the fabric as a quilting guide. Remove the safety pins as you sew to them.

- Quilt on a flat surface.

Practice Machine Quilting

Cut a 10" by 15" piece of fabric. Cut a 10" by 15" piece of flannel. Pin-baste the panels to the flannel batting, using a size 0 safety pin. Pin every 2 to 3". Remove the pins as you sew to them.

Use a darning foot for free-motion quilting. Use a walking foot for straight line quilting.

Stipple Quilting

Place a darning foot on the machine. Lower the feed dogs. Place the sample under the darning foot. Stipple quilt half of the sample, following the guidelines on page 15.

Straight Line Quilting

Place a walking foot on the machine. Raise the feed dogs. Practice straight line quilting on half of the sample.

You do not need to mark lines on the fabric. Try to straight line quilt without using lines.

Quilt straight diagonal lines in one direction, and then in the opposite direction. Do not sew back and forth, as this pulls the fabric.

Practice Sample

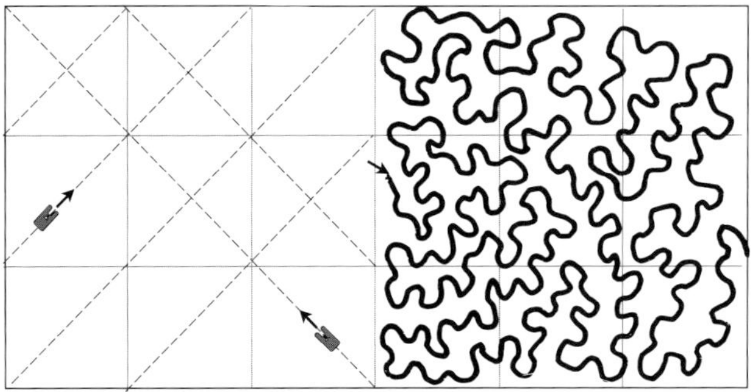

Straight Line Quilting   Stipple Quilting

The stipple quilting pictured on the right half of the practice sample is done by "free-motion" quilting, which is hand guided by you. The straight line quilting is done without lines to follow. Draw lines with a ruler if you need them as a guide.

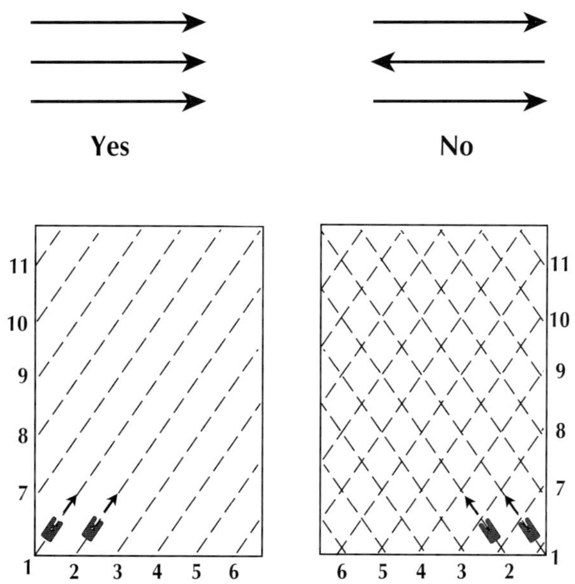

Stipple Quilting by Machine

Safety-pin-baste the panels to the flannel batting, using size 0 safety pins. Pin every 2" to 3", or use the "Quilter's Basting Gun"® if you prefer.

Use 100% cotton thread on the top and in the bobbin; then try monofilament or clear thread on the top and 100% cotton thread in the bobbin. Use a darning foot. You can also try a "topstitch needle" with a metallic thread.

Lower the teeth of the feed dogs. Quilt on a flat surface. **Quilt from the center out.** Work in small areas. Develop a steady rhythm. The needle sews fast, and the hands move slowly.

Try to quilt continuous lines, not crossing back over the lines.

Draw this with a pencil on paper first.

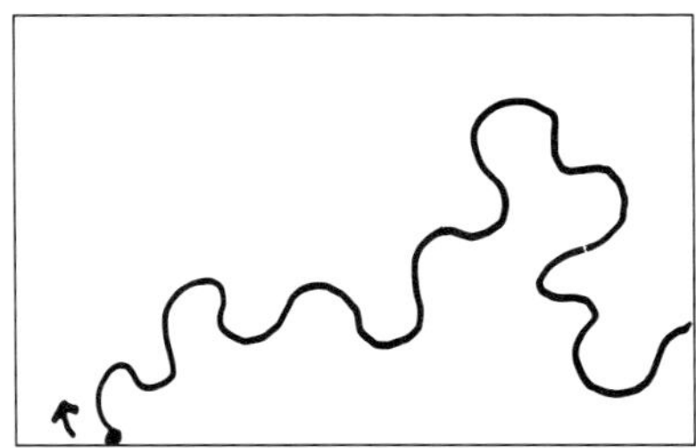

Copy this with a pencil

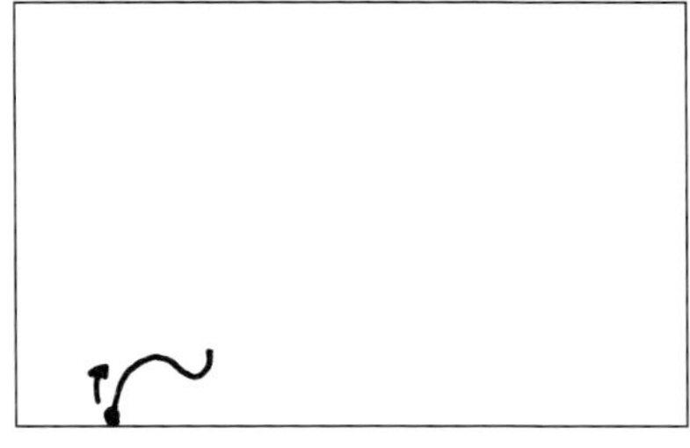

Draw here

Quilt out from the center. Quilt one quarter of the panel; then go back to the center and quilt the next section, as illustrated below.

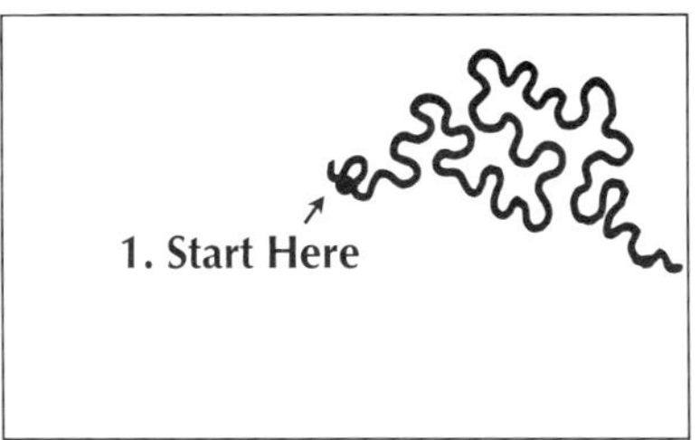

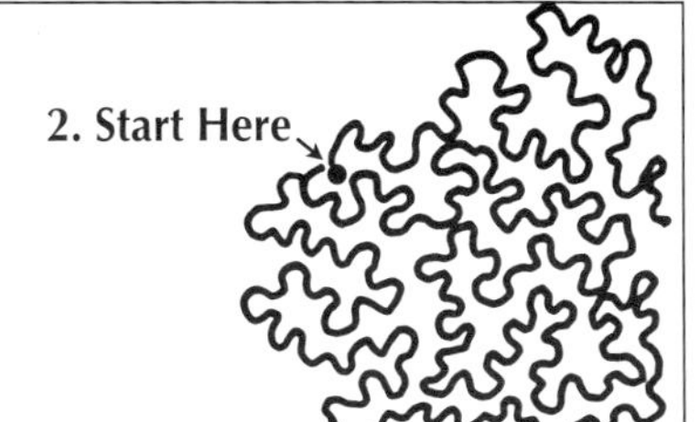

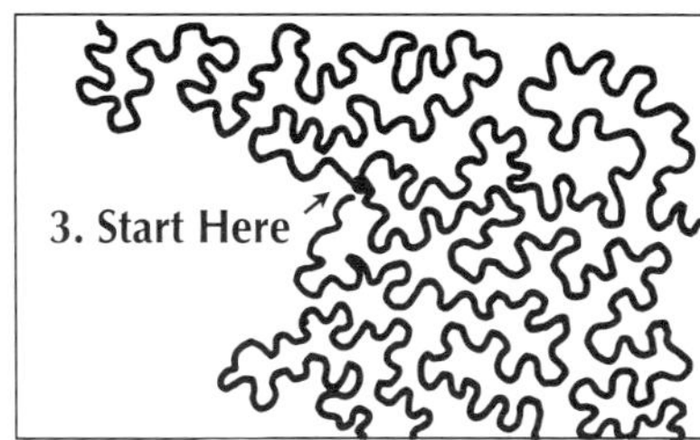

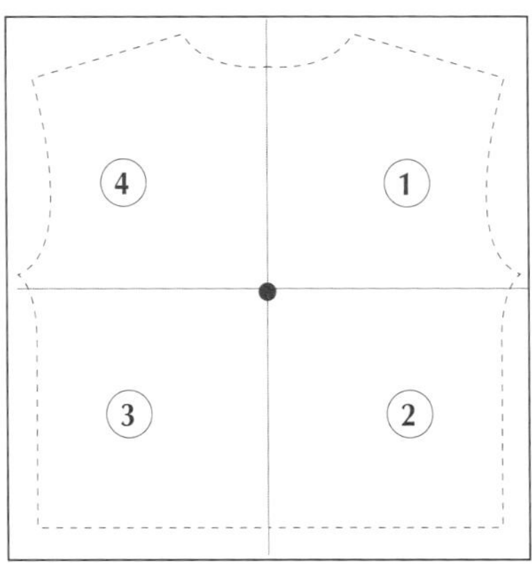

Stipple quilting.

Pieced front panels.

Body Measurements

SIZE	Petite	Small	Medium	Large	X-Large
	(4-6)	(8-10)	(12-14)	(16-18)	(20-22)
Bust	28-33	34-36	37-41	42-44	45-50
Hip	32-35	36-38	39-45	46-52	53-56
Pattern Hip Measurement	43"	47"	51"	57"	62"
Back length (neck to hip)	23"	23"	25"	27"	29"

★**Tip:** Cut your size out of muslin and try it on before cutting the jacket pieces.

Cut the elastic for the bottom of the jacket 6" less than your hip measurement.

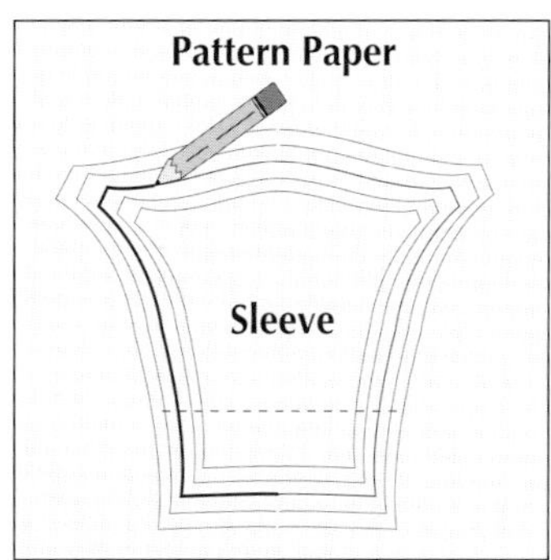

Find the lines marking your size.

The heavy line is the cutting line. Mark over the lines for your size with a red felt marker or a colored pencil. Place the pattern paper over the master pattern. Trace your size onto a piece of pattern paper.

Antiquing the Fabric— Making the Fabric Look Like an "Old" Quilt

For an antique look to your fabric, wash the panels. Do not cut the jacket parts until these panels have been shrunk.

The panels include the extra yardage that will shrink in washing and drying. Serge or zigzag around the outer edges of the flannel rectangles to reduce fraying. Be careful not to serge or cut into the pieced squares more than ⅛".

Place all the quilted panels in the washing machine. Wash in lukewarm water, using a little pure soap if desired. Orvus "Quiltsoap" is a pure soap designed for fine cottons.

Dry your fabric in the dryer on warm. Place a large, dry towel in the dryer to absorb moisture and help to soften the tumbling action of the dryer.

Repeat for a more wrinkled look.

Steam press the panels if needed.

The quilted fabric panels are now ready to cut into the jacket

Determining Your Size

This jacket is loose fitting. It should close and button at the bottom. The pattern is adjustable to your height and sleeve length and includes petite and larger sizes. Measure your hip and find the size on the chart at left.

The hip measurement of the pattern should be 6"± larger than your hip measurement to allow for the ease. For example, if your hip measures 43", choose the Medium pattern size, which means that the bottom edge of the pattern should measure 49"±.

The secret of the fit is in the hip; if your hip measurement is larger than indicated for your recommended size, you may taper the side seams out from the armhole to add for the extra fullness.

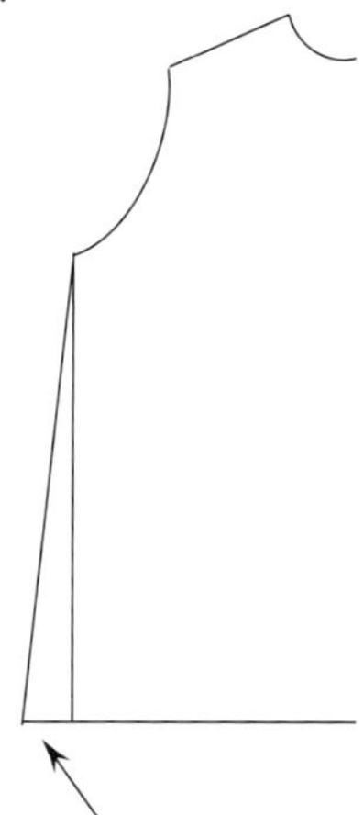

For example, if your hip measurement is 49", but your bust measurement goes with a 43" hip, add 1" to each side seam at the bottom edge and taper to the armhole.

Using the Multi-size Pattern and Making the Paper Pattern

Pattern Markings

— — Place on fold. Place "fold line" indicated on pattern on the folded edge of the fabric.

The seam line includes a ½" seam allowance on all pieces.

——— The cutting line is indicated by a thick black line on the pattern paper.

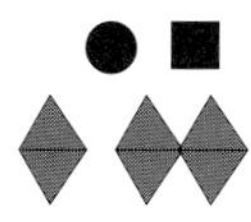

Match marks are used to align corresponding areas of the pattern pieces, such as pockets, sleeves, bands, and seams. Transfer these marks from the pattern to the fabric, using a wash-out pen or colored pencil.

– – – – Lengthen or shorten line

You may need to lengthen or shorten the jacket front, back, and sleeve. To determine the length that you want, measure from the back of your neck to where you want the bottom edge of the jacket to be. Make a note of this measurement. Measure the pattern from the neck edge to the bottom edge. Cut the pattern on the mark provided to lengthen or shorten to your measurement.

Measure the sleeve length from the top of the arm to the edge of the sleeve. Adjust the pattern to the length needed.

Trace the pattern onto lightweight interfacing or paper.
Cut out the traced pattern parts. Transfer all match marks, notches, and numbers onto the pattern.

Transfer the markings
Transfer all match marks indicated on the pattern piece to the jacket parts. Use a colored pencil or a wash-out pen to mark the fabric.

Pattern Pieces

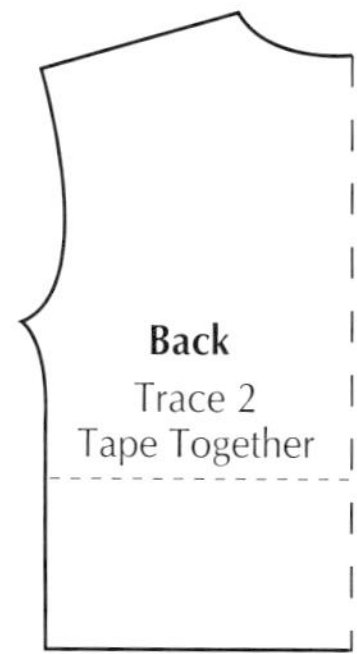

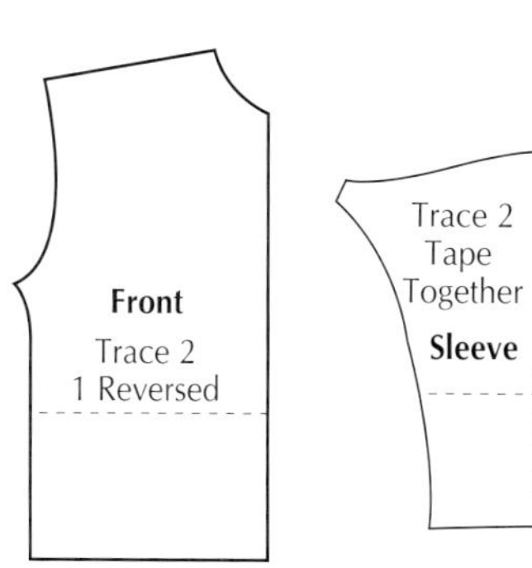

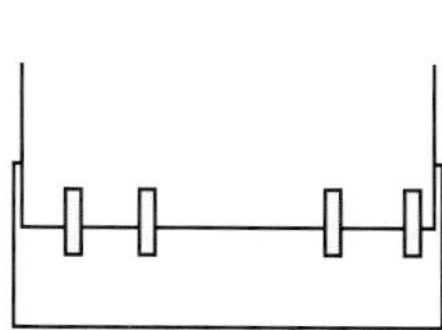

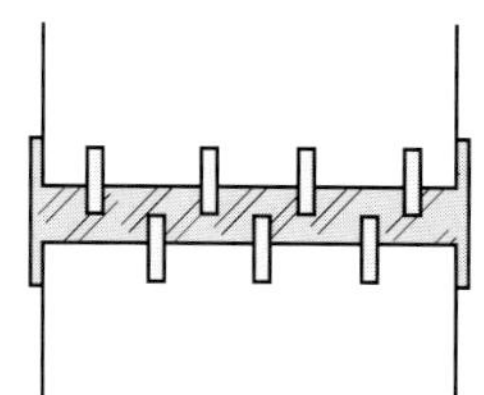

Overlap the pattern pieces to shorten. Spread the pattern apart and add a piece of paper to lengthen. Tape the paper together.

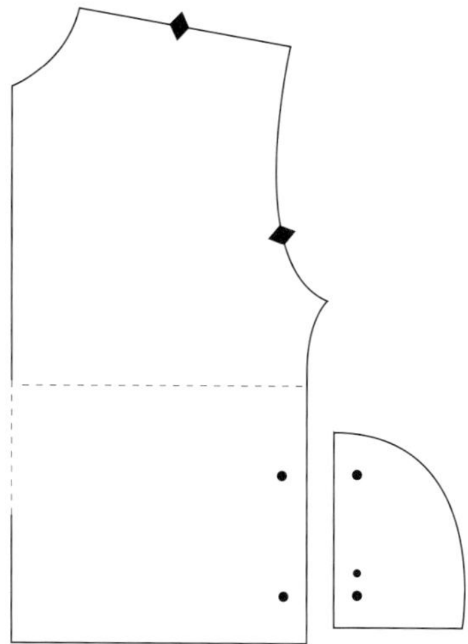

Cutting the Jacket Parts

- Pin the paper pattern pieces on the right side of the quilted panels.

- Align the bottom of the pattern exactly along the bottom edge of the bottom row of squares.

- Do not cut any of the fabric off the bottom of the 2" squares. There is a maximum ⅜" to ½" seam allowance at the bottom edge of the squares.

- Carefully cut out the jacket parts.

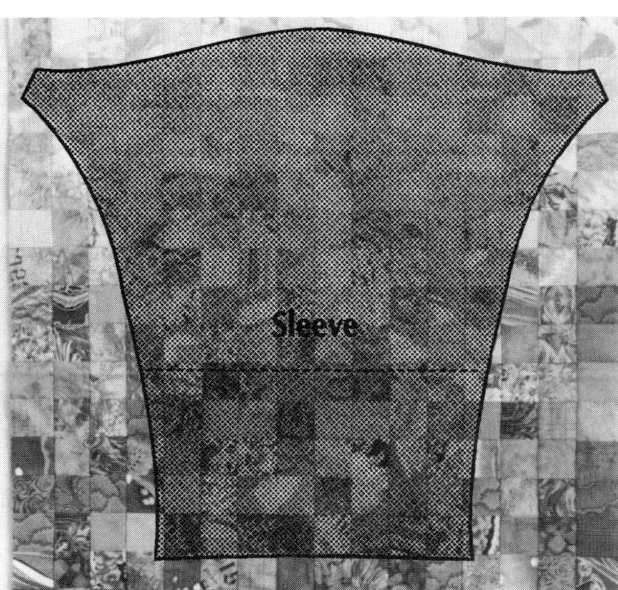

Sleeve pattern pieces positioned on sleeve panels.

Jacket Assembly

Pin and sew the parts together following these directions.

It may be necessary to use a walking foot to assemble bulky fabrics. If you have a serger, use it for most of the jacket assembly.

Use the diagrams as a guide for placement and sewing the pieces.

Collar

The collar is the first part of the jacket that you assemble because it has to be sewn into the neckline as soon as you sew the shoulder seams together.

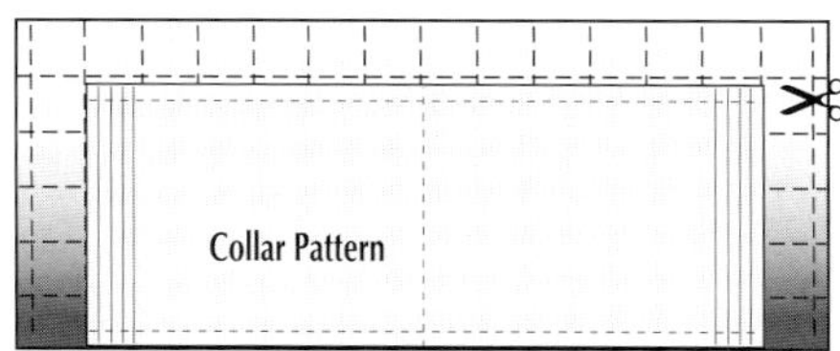

Place the pattern piece over the right side of the quilted collar. Align the pattern with one edge of the quilted collar. Cut the collar.

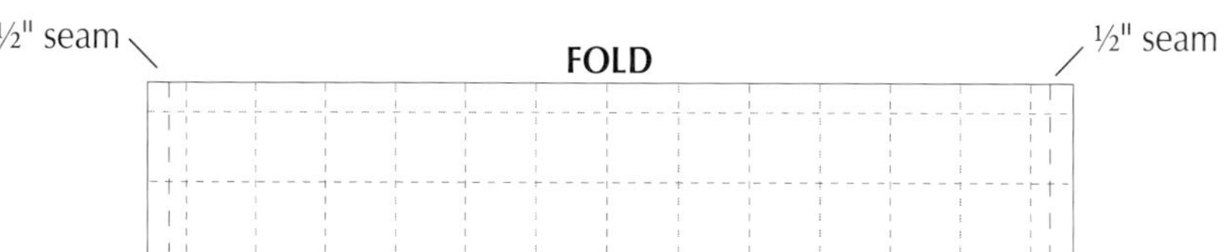

Fold right sides together and sew ½" from the edges.

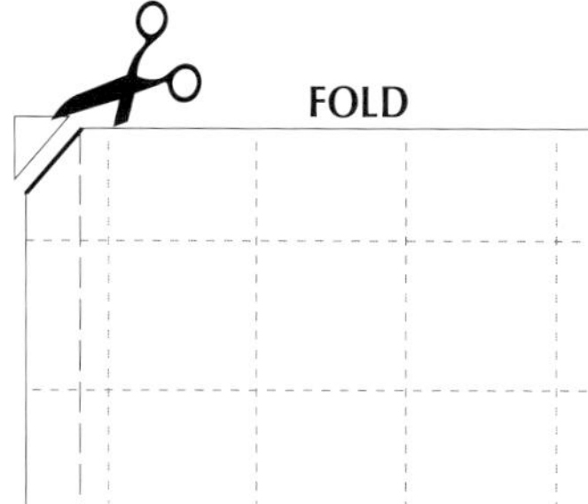

Trim the corners of the folded edge.

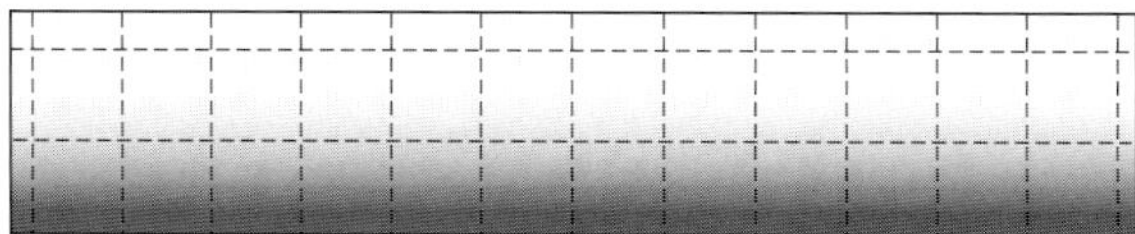

Turn the collar right side out. Make sharp, square points by using a pointed (but not sharp) tool to poke the corners out.

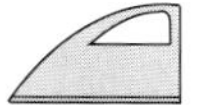

Press the collar.

Sewing the Fronts and Back Together

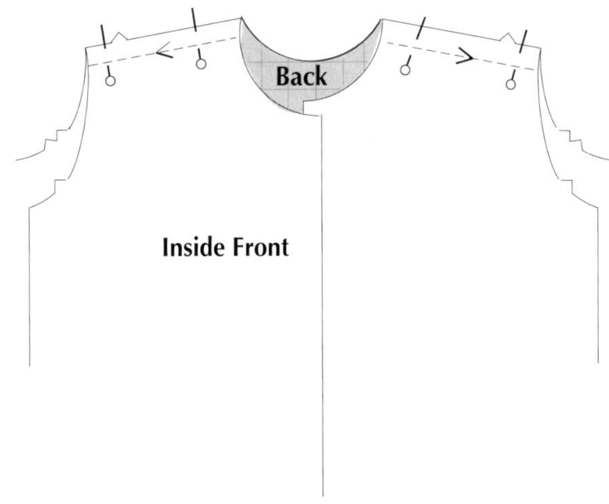

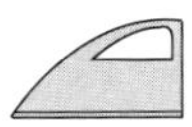

☐ Pin and sew or serge **Fronts and Back** together at the shoulder seams, right sides together, using a ½" seam.

Press shoulder seams open and flat (if not serged).

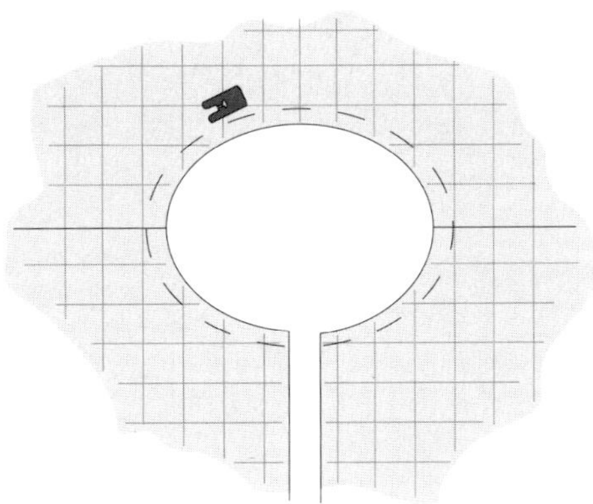

☐ Staystitch ⅜" around the neck edge using a basting stitch.

Attaching the Collar

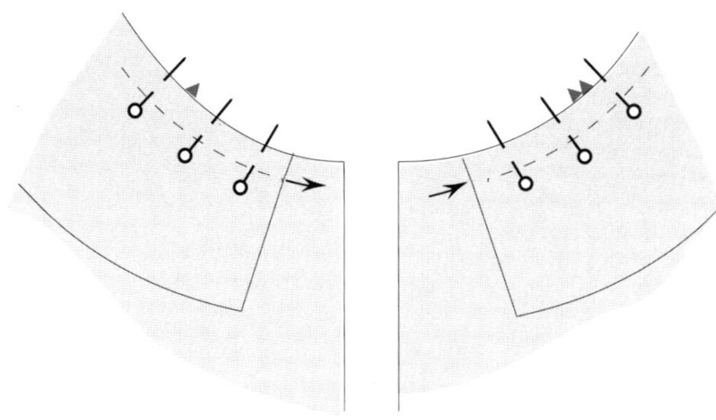

☐ Pin the collar to the neck edge. Match all marks.

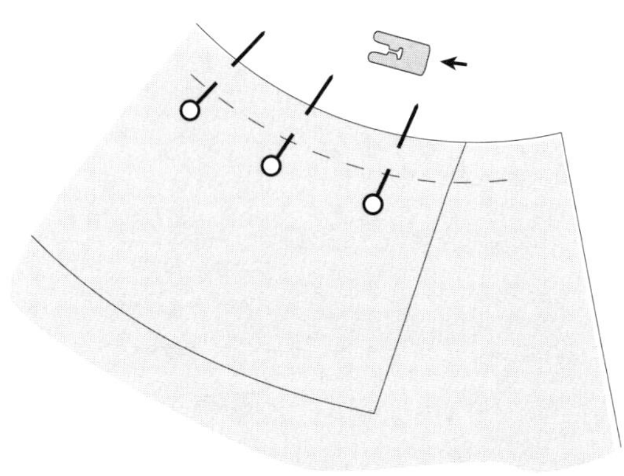

☐ Sew ½" from the neck edge, removing the pins as you sew to them.

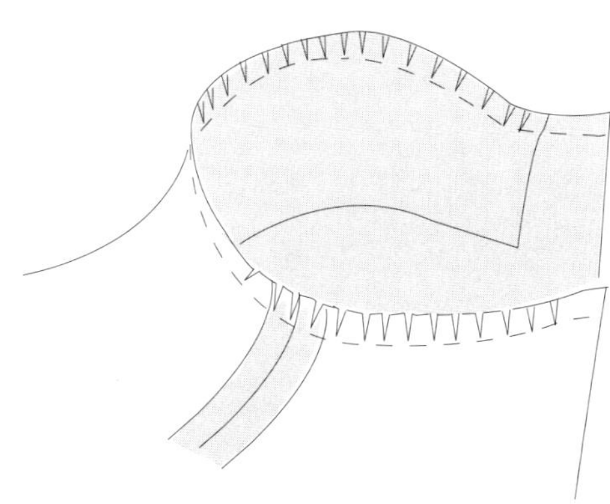

☐ Use very sharp scissors to clip the neck seam allowance every ½".

Clip very close to the seam, but be careful not to clip the seam.

Sleeves

☐ Staystich ⅜" from sleeve edge, using a long basting stitch.

☐ With **Right Sides Together,** pin sleeve to jacket armhole.

Match large dot ● at sleeve head to dot at shoulder seam.

Match notch marks of sleeve to notch marks of armhole.

Pin the sleeve to the armhole.

Pull the basting stitches between dots to ease the fullness of the sleeve to fit the armhole.

Pin every ½" to 1".

☐ Sew or serge the sleeve to the armhole, using a ½" seam.

☐ Use very sharp scissors to clip the seam allowance every ½".

Clip very close to the seam, but be careful not to clip into the seam.

☐ Trim excess seam allowance.

🔸 Press the seam toward the sleeve.

Pockets

☐ Cut the pockets from the lining fabric.

☐ Match dots of pocket pieces to **front** side seams and pin.

☐ Stitch one pocket to front at each side, using a ⅜" seam.

🔸 Press the seams toward the pockets.

☐ Match dots of pocket pieces to **back** side seams and pin.

Stitch one pocket to each back side, using a ⅜" seam.

🔸 Press the seams toward the pockets.

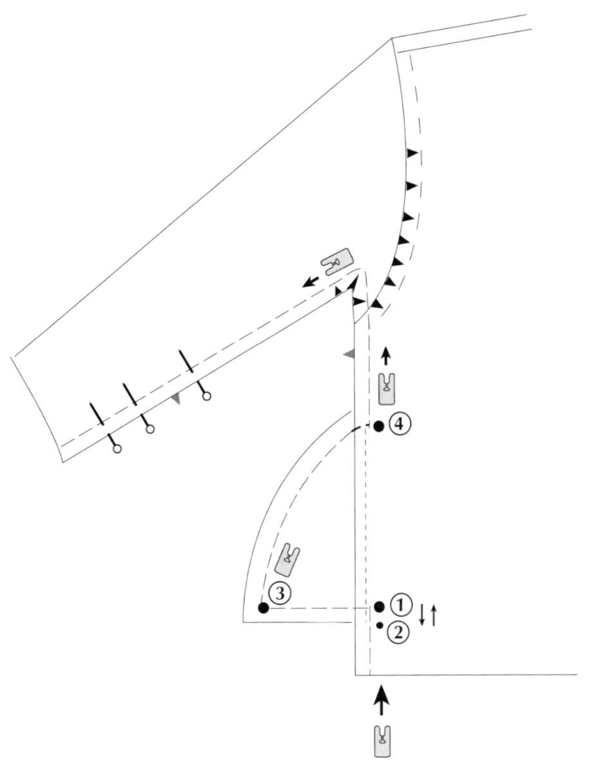

Side Seams

Match markings of front and back together at sides and pin.

Pin sleeve edges together.

Pin pockets together.

Sew ½" seam beginning at the jacket bottom edge to dot ●#1 below pocket.

Backstitch to small dot ●#2.

Pivot and sew lower pocket edge to dot ●#3.

Pivot and sew to dot ●#4.

Sew from dot ●#4 to sleeve edge, pivoting at armhole.

Clip to seam at dot ●#4.

Clip the underarm seam every ½", or as needed.

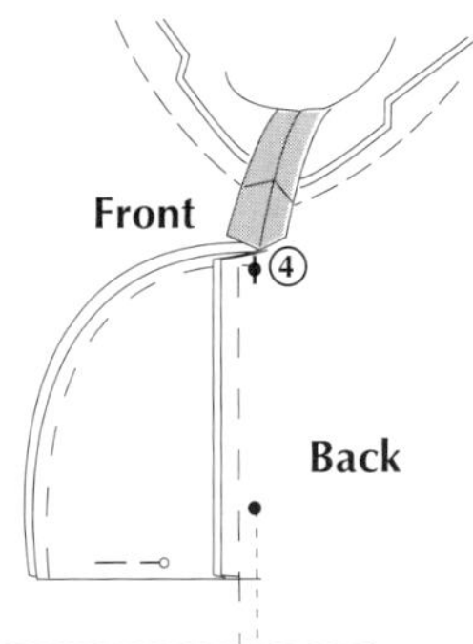

Serge seam from dot ●#4 to sleeve end if you are using a serger.

Turn and press the pockets toward front and pin.

Shoulder Pads (optional)

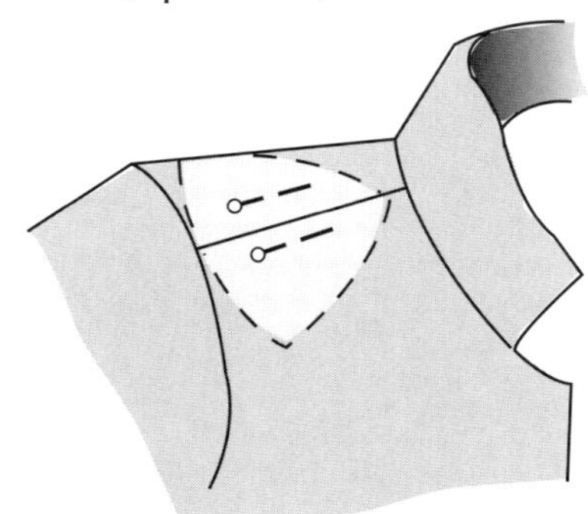

Try on your jacket.

Place the shoulder pads in the seam line, and adjust them to your fit.

Pin the shoulder pads from the outside.

Turn the jacket inside-out.

Hand stitch the shoulder pads to the inside shoulder seam.

General Instructions for Lining and Finishing the Jacket

To finish the jacket, sew the lining to the neckline, right sides together. Carefully clip and trim the neckline.

With the jacket inside out, sew the lining to the edge of the right front band and to the edge of the left front jacket. Fold the band, right sides together, along the fold line, and sew the neck edge. Sew the right neckline edge, and then sew the left front neckline edge.

While the jacket is still inside out, sew the bottom elastic to the fronts, 3" from the front edges at the bottom edge. Sew the bottom front edges from the front edges to, and across the side seams. Turn the jacket right side out through the bottom edge opening.

Press the edges. Position the elastic along the bottom edge and topstitch above, below, and in the middle of the elastic.

Topstitch the jacket edges. Pull the elastic through the sleeves and topstitch.

To finish the jacket, make the buttonholes and hand sew the buttons in place.

Lining Pattern Pieces

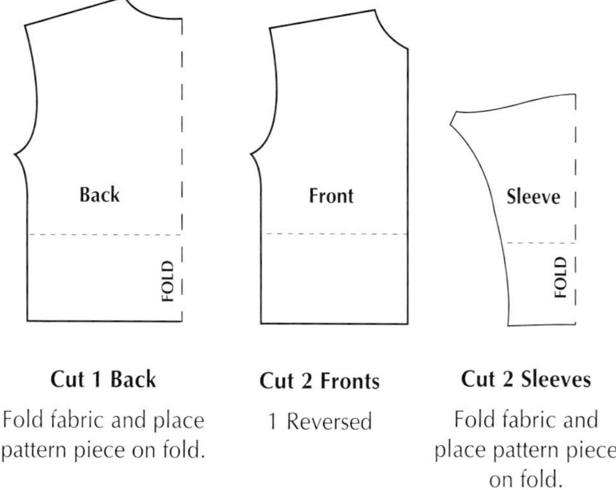

Cut 1 Back
Fold fabric and place pattern piece on fold.

Cut 2 Fronts
1 Reversed

Cut 2 Sleeves
Fold fabric and place pattern piece on fold.

The lining pattern pieces should be the same size as the finished jacket parts.

Lengthen or shorten as necessary.

Cut the pockets according to the directions on page 21.

Jacket Lining Cutting Diagram

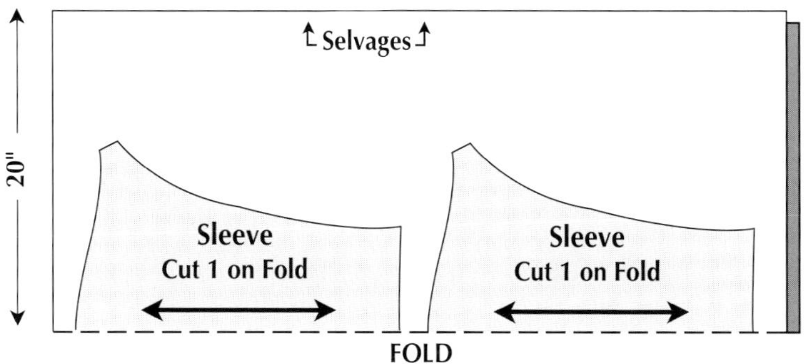

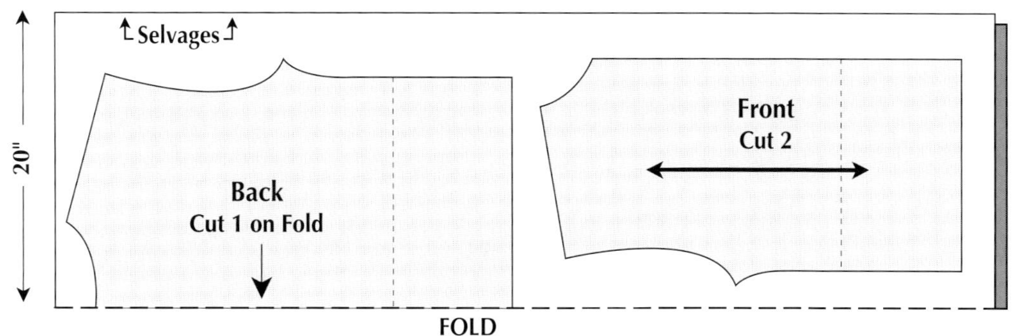

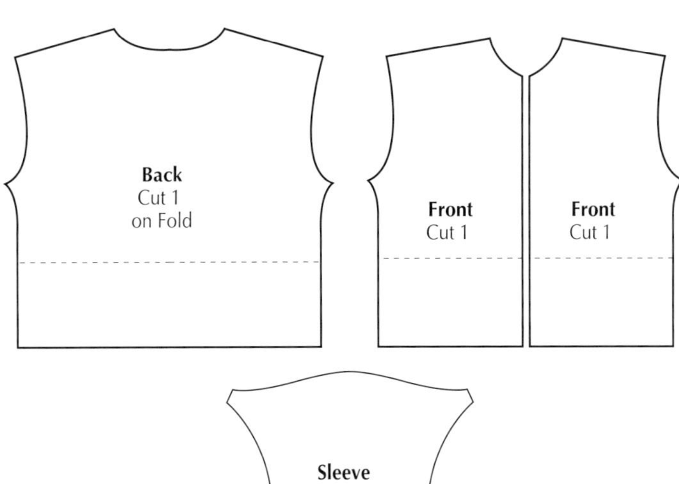

Lining Assembly

Do not cut the lining until you have sewn, washed, and cut the outer jacket parts.

Cut the lining exactly the same size as the **trimmed outer jacket parts.** You may use the trimmed outer jacket parts for the front, back, and sleeves as pattern templates.

Sew the pockets to the jacket. Assemble the lining: sew fronts to back, sleeves sewn to armhole, and sew the side seams together.

Sew the collar to the outer jacket, and sew the lining to the jacket at the neck line.

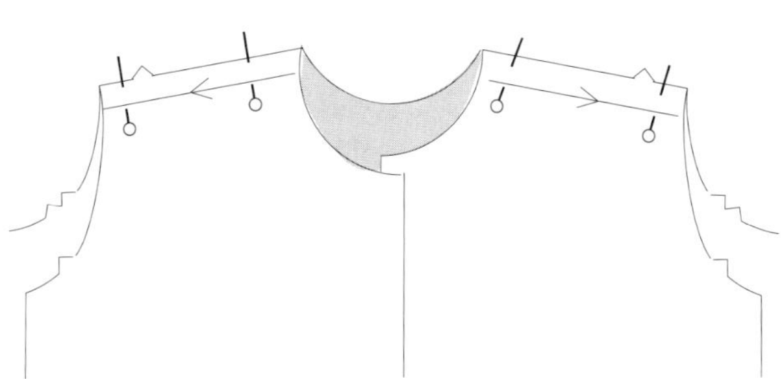

Pin and sew or serge **Fronts and Back** together at shoulders, right sides together, using a ½" seam.

Press the shoulder seams open and flat (if not serged).

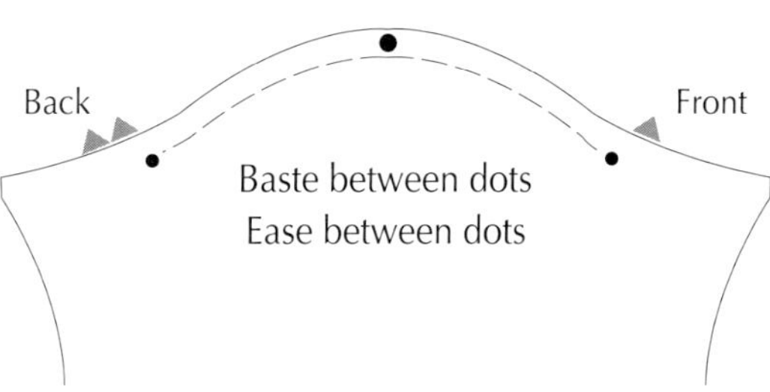

Sew a basting stitch at the sleeve head between the two smaller dots.

Pin the sleeve to the armhole.

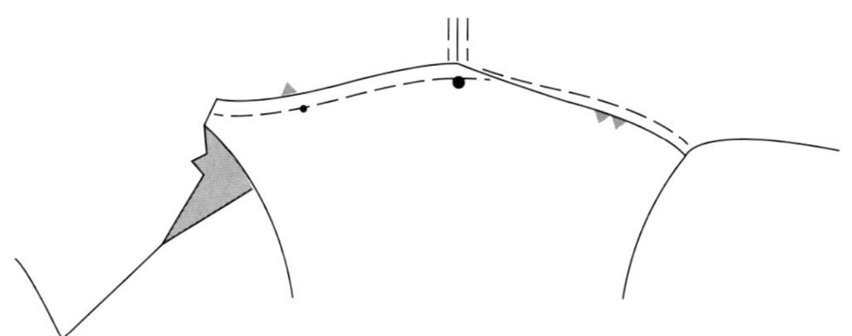

☐ Ease the sleeve to the armhole between the dots.

Sew or serge the sleeve to the armhole, using a ½" seam.

☐ Clip the shoulder seam every ¼" to ½", being careful not clip into seam line.

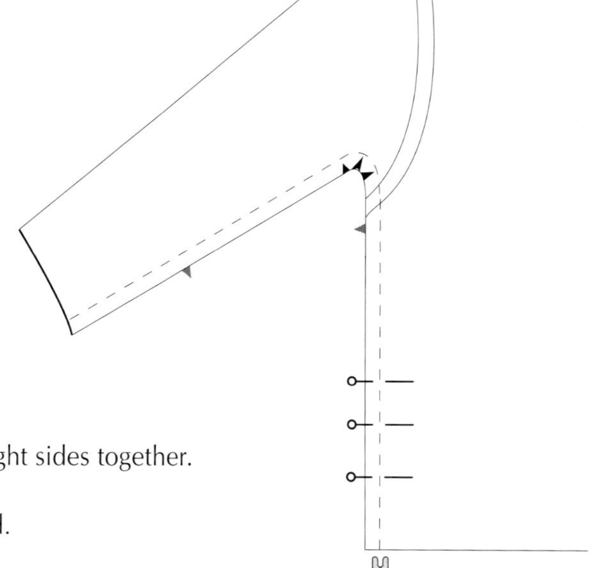

☐ Pin the side seams of the lining, right sides together.
Sew or serge, using a ½" seam.
Clip the underarm seam as needed.

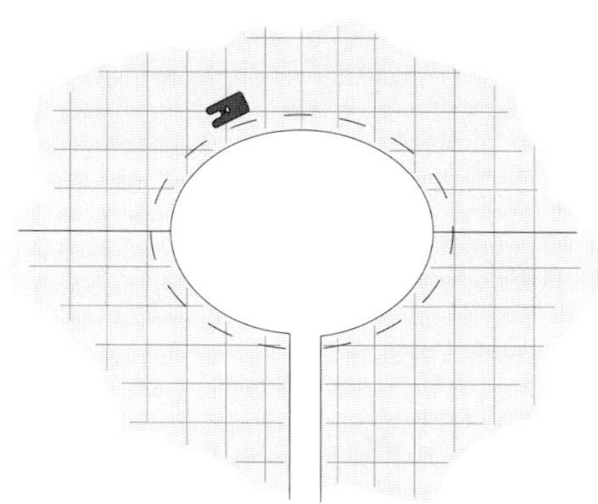

☐ Staystitch ⅜" around the neck edge, using a long basting stitch.

Creating the Front Bands

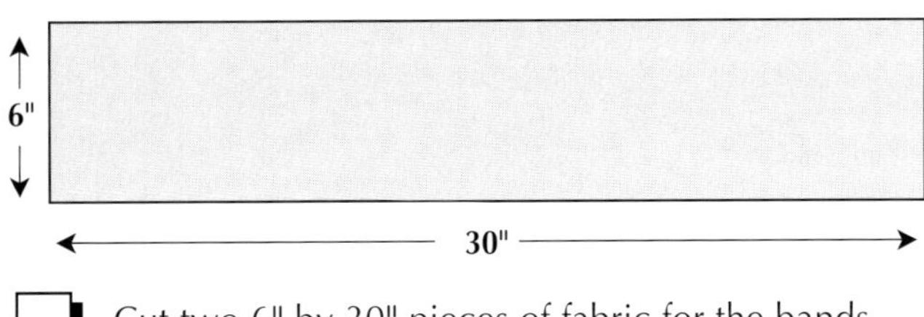

☐ Cut two 6" by 30" pieces of fabric for the bands.

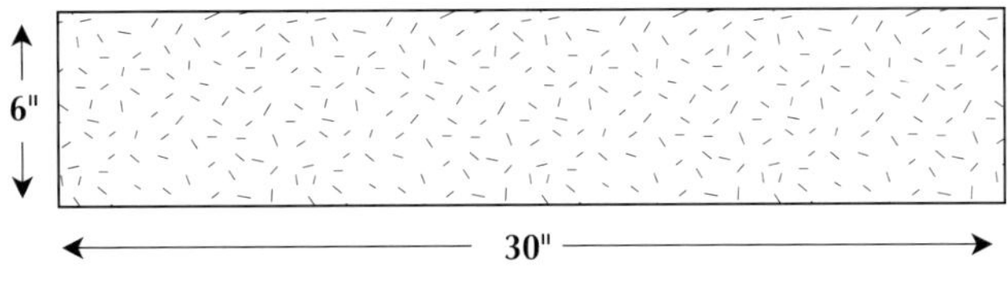

☐ Cut two 6" by 30" pieces of flannel.

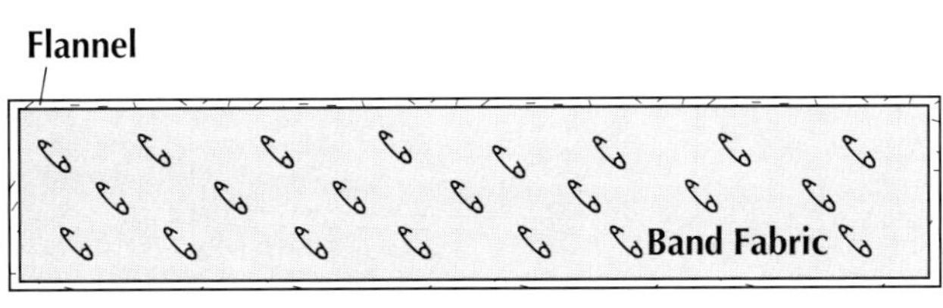

☐ Safety pin the front bands to the flannel.
Pin every 2" to 3".

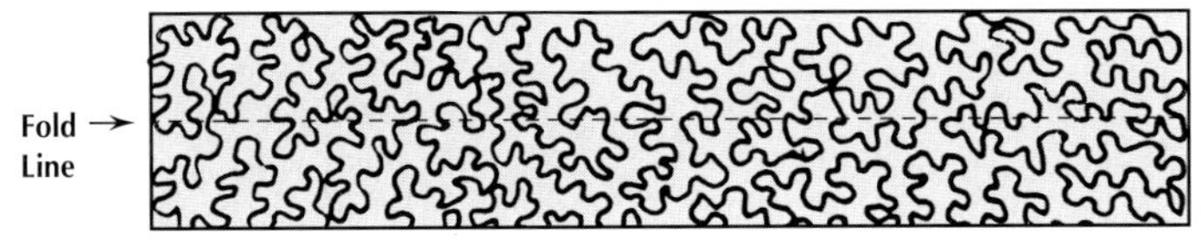

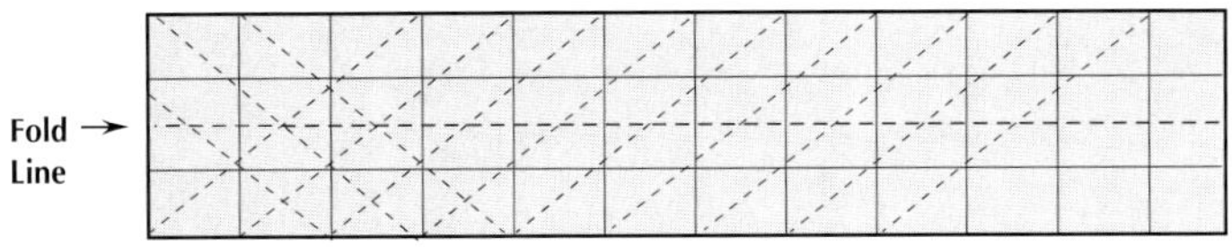

☐ Machine quilt the front bands, using stipple or straight line quilting. See the practice sample on page 10.

☐ Wash and dry the bands to shrink and antique.

Fitting the Front Bands to the Jacket Front

The bands are re-cut from the larger quilted band to fit the length of your jacket.

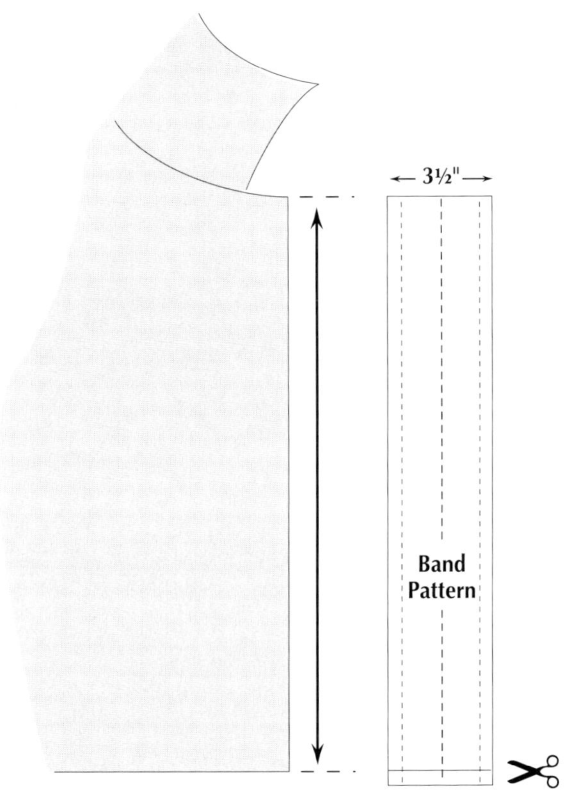

☐ Use the front band pattern.

☐ Measure the jacket from the neckline to the bottom front edge.

The pattern should be the same length as the front edge. Adjust the band pattern to fit the front edge length.

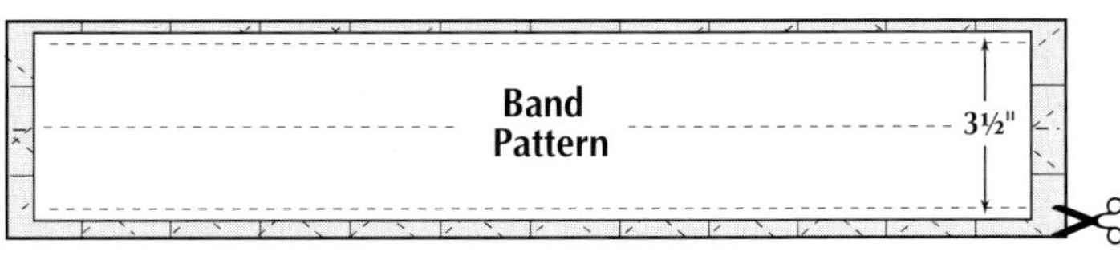

☐ Cut two bands.

Sewing the Lining to the Neck

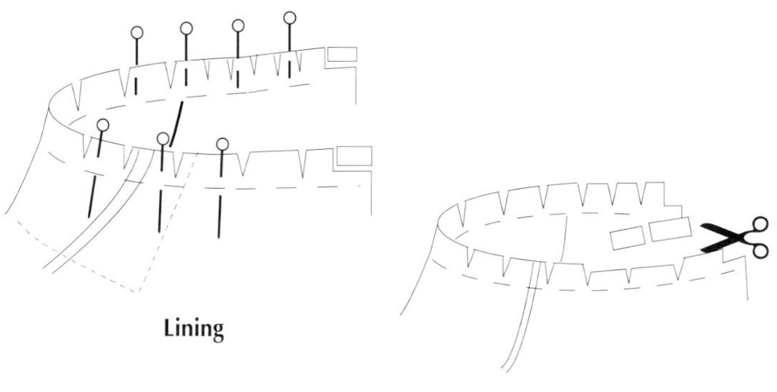

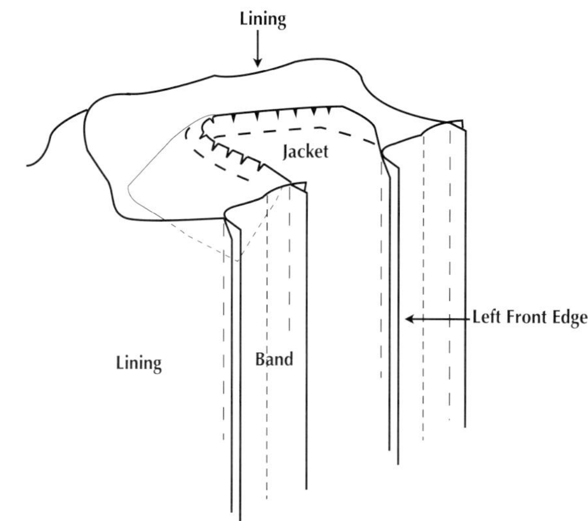

☐ Pin the lining over the collar, **Right Sides Together,** matching raw edges at the neck line.

Match dots at the neckline and shoulder seam lines.

Pin every ½".

Sew ½" from neckline edge.

☐ Clip every ½" around the neck edge, being careful not to cut the seam.

Trim seam to ⅛".

☐ Pin and sew the lining to the right front band edge, right sides together, using a ½" seam allowance.

☐ Pin and sew the lining to the left front band edge, right sides together, using a ½" seam allowance.

Sewing the Front Bands

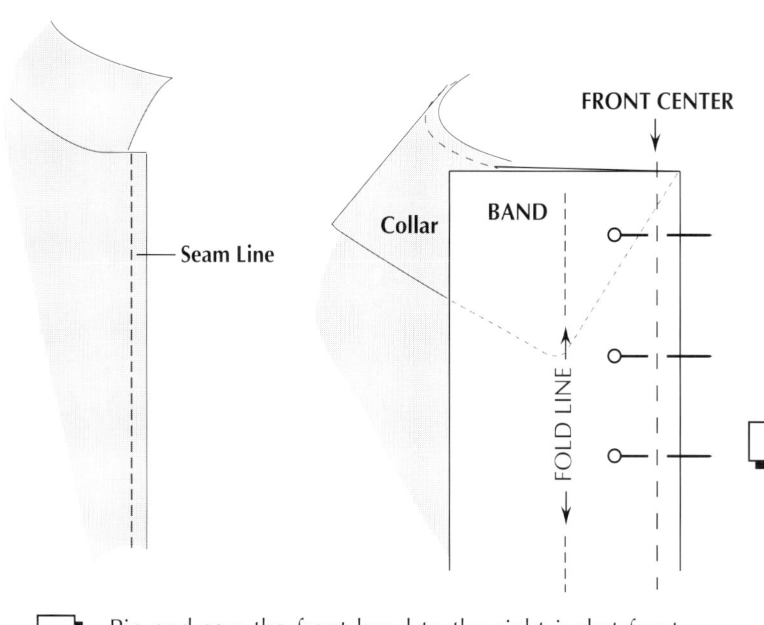

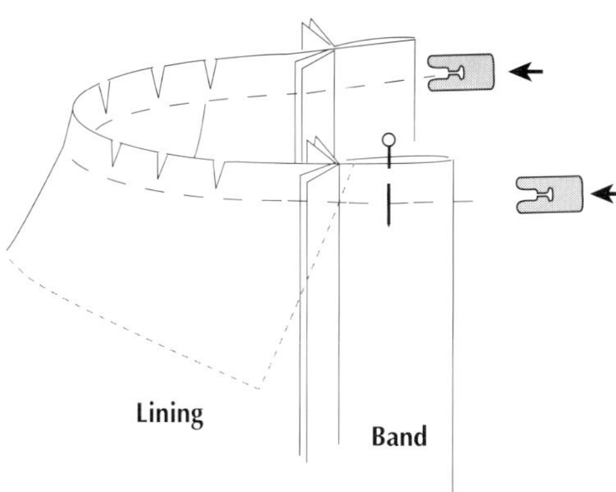

☐ Pin and sew the front band to the right jacket front edge, right sides together, using a ½" seam allowance.

☐ Pin and sew the front band to the left jacket front edge, using a ½" seam allowance.

☐ Fold the right front band along the center fold line, right sides together.

Pin along the neck edges.

Sew neckline from the front edge to the collar seam line, using a ½" seam.

Fold the left front band along the center fold line, right sides together.

Pin along the neckline edge.

Sew the neckline from the front edge to the collar seam line.

Adding the Elastic at the Hemline

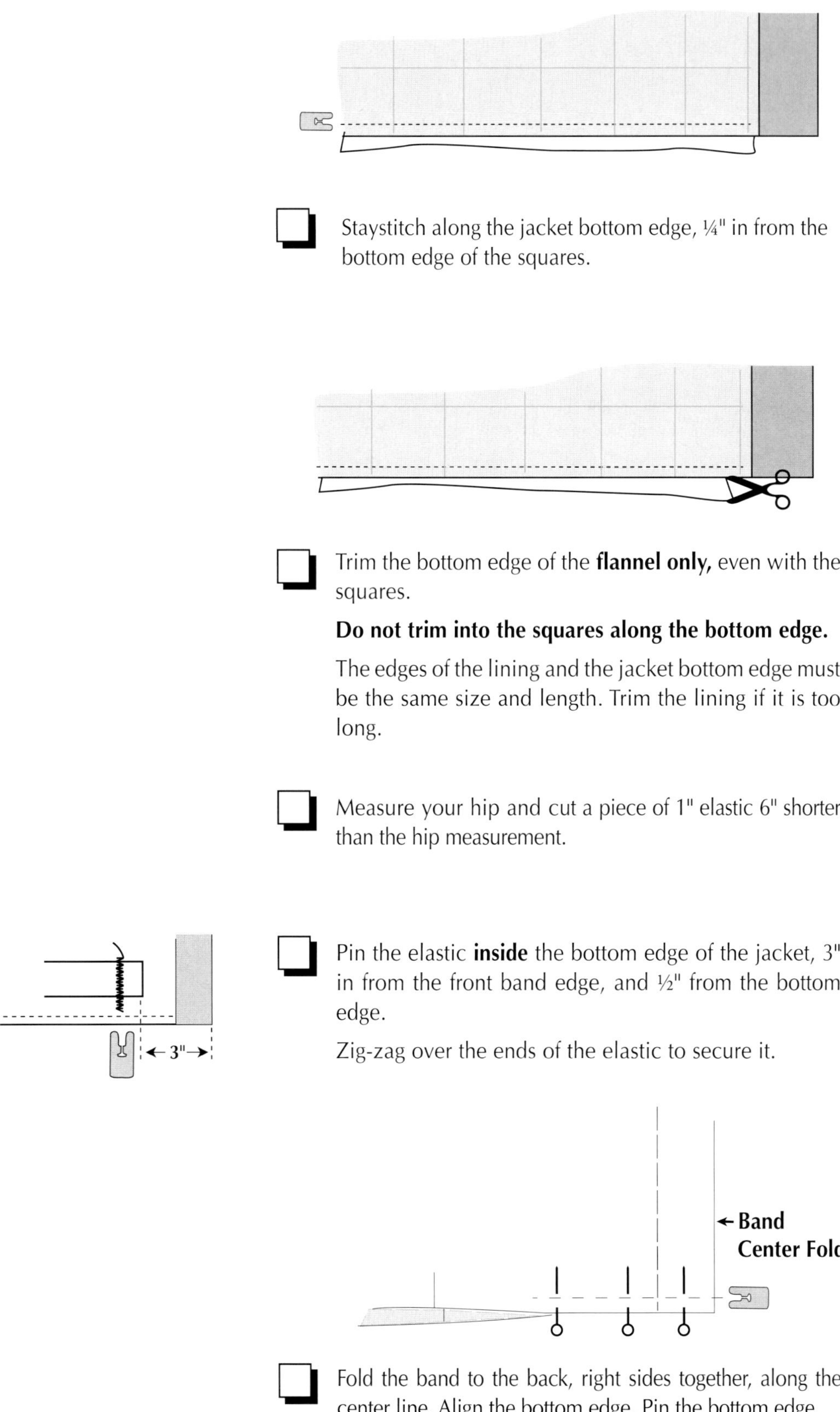

Staystitch along the jacket bottom edge, ¼" in from the bottom edge of the squares.

Trim the bottom edge of the **flannel only,** even with the squares.

Do not trim into the squares along the bottom edge.

The edges of the lining and the jacket bottom edge must be the same size and length. Trim the lining if it is too long.

Measure your hip and cut a piece of 1" elastic 6" shorter than the hip measurement.

Pin the elastic **inside** the bottom edge of the jacket, 3" in from the front band edge, and ½" from the bottom edge.

Zig-zag over the ends of the elastic to secure it.

Fold the band to the back, right sides together, along the center line. Align the bottom edge. Pin the bottom edge.

Sew from the folded band edge to across the side seams, ½" from the bottom edge.

Sew from the left front edge to across the side seams, ½" from the bottom edge.

Leave Open

Leave 8" to 10" open at the back bottom edge.

The jacket and the lining are rights sides together. The collar is inside, between the jacket and the lining.

Turn the jacket right side out through the opening at the bottom edge.

Poke out all corners.
Press all edges.

Fold the bottom edge of the jacket seam allowance to the inside.

Fold the lining seam allowance to the inside.

Pin the back bottom lining edge to the jacket edge along the opening at the bottom edge.

Hand sew the hem opening of the lining closed.
Pull the elastic flat and straight along the bottom.
Ease the jacket to the elastic.

Pin the elastic securely in place along the bottom edge.

Topstitch along the top edge of the elastic. Stretch and sew to fit. Remove the pins. Topstitch along the bottom edge of the elastic, being careful not to catch the elastic in the stitching.
Topstitch along the center of the elastic.

Sew the back opening ⅛" from the bottom edge.

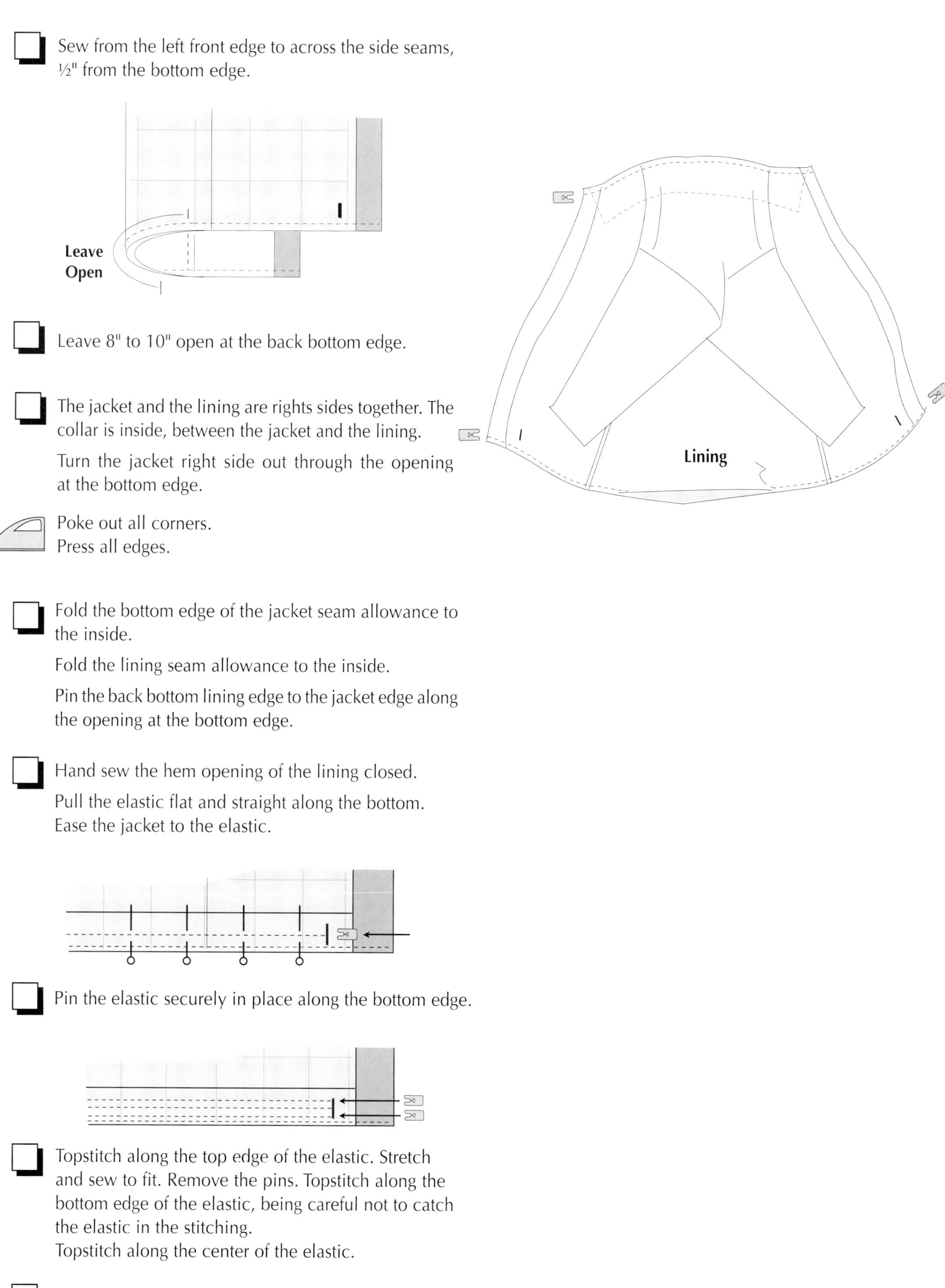

Sleeve Elastic

☐ Measure your wrist and add 1".

Cut two pieces of 1" wide elastic to this measurement.

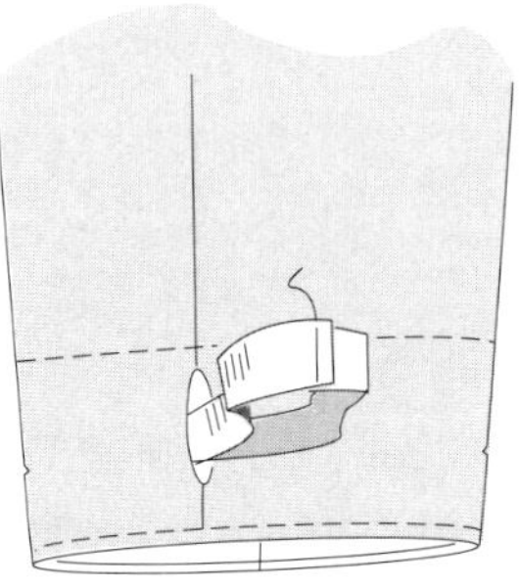

☐ Bring the sleeve lining down to the sleeve edge to form the casing for the elastic. Turn ½" of the lower edge of the lining to the inside.

Turn ½" of the sleeve edge to the inside.

Press, pin, and topstitch ¼" from the edge.

☐ Make a casing for the elastic by sewing one seam 1⅜" from the bottom topstitching.

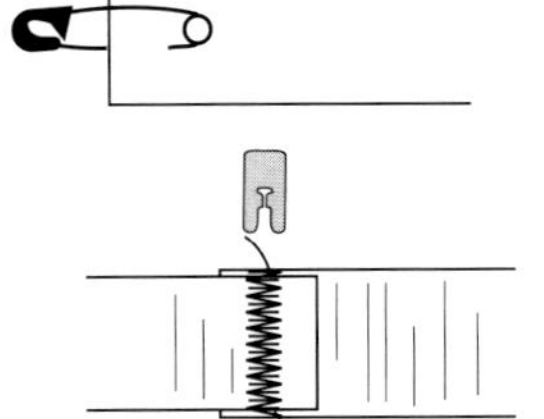

☐ Open the lining seam and use a size 3 safety pin to feed the elastic through the opening.

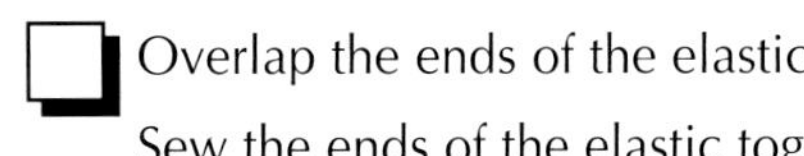

☐ Overlap the ends of the elastic.

Sew the ends of the elastic together by hand or machine.

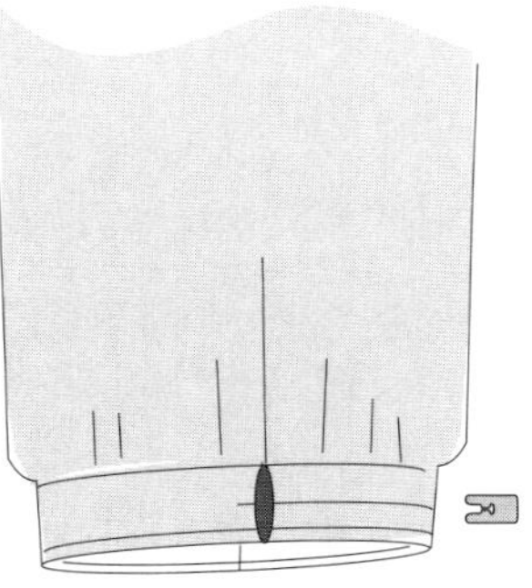

☐ Adjust the fullness, and stitch the opening closed by hand.

Machine topstitch over the center of the elastic.

Buttonholes

- Use a wash-out blue pen to mark the buttonhole placement.

- Measure ½" from the top and bottom edges, and make marks for the top and bottom buttonholes.

- Measure between the buttonholes, divide evenly for three or four more buttonholes, and mark the rest of the buttonholes.

- Make the buttonholes, using a walking foot on thick fabrics. Adjust the length of the buttonhole for the size of button you are using.

- Sew on the buttons.

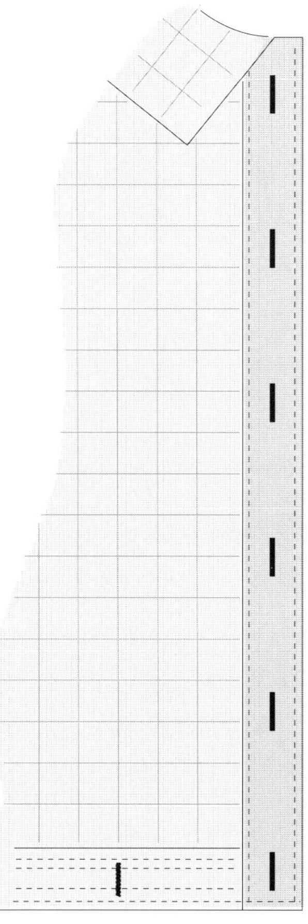
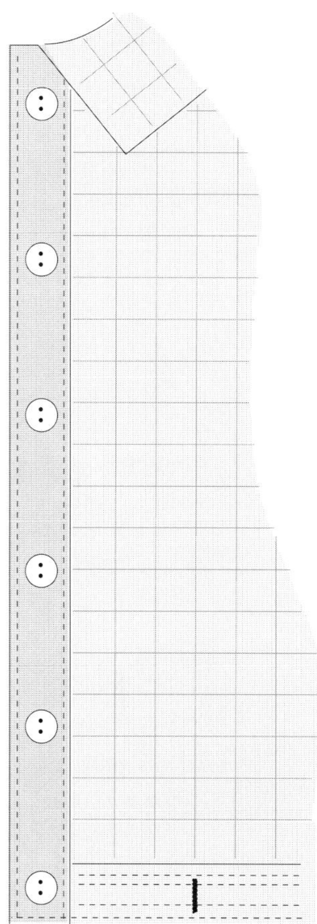

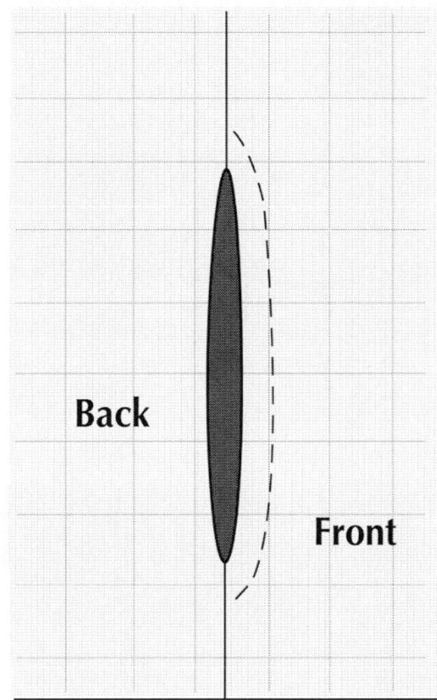

- Topstitch the front pocket edges by hand or machine if desired.

- Press the entire jacket.

You've done it. Try on your completed jacket and admire!

The New Sampler Quilt
Diana Leone
Perfect bound $19.95
Comb bound $24.95
German ed. $39.95
Full-size Quilt Designs $3.98

Basic Seminole Patchwork
Cheryl Bradkin
$16.95

Attic Windows
Diana Leone
$16.95

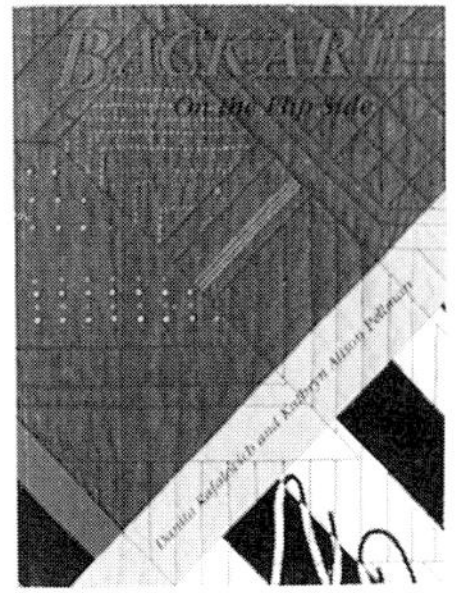

Backart
Rafalovich & Pellman
$19.95

The Quiltmaker's Handbook

The 2nd Quiltmaker's Handbook
Michael James
$14.95 each

Quiltmaker's Book of 6" Patterns
Anthony & Lehman
$12.95

Morning Star Quilts
Florence Pulford
Soft cover $24.95
Hard cover $34.95

Mini Appliqued Hearts
Sondra Rudey
$2.50

The Tied Quilt
Diana Leone
$2.50

Buyer's Source

Watercolor Packets
50 6½" florals $29.95 each
Request pack 1, 2, 3 or 4; each is different.

For all items mentioned in this book, write to:

Mail Order
The Quilting Bee, Dept. WC
357 Castro Street, Mtn. View, CA 94041 USA (415) 969-1714
Leone Publications office: (415) 965-9797 Fax: (415) 965-9799

Visit The Quilting Bee in Mountain View, when you are in Northern California, USA.

This store, owned by Diana Leone, carries a wide variety of products for the quilter.

If there is something that you want, just write to us, and we will advise you as to price and availability.

Mail Today
**To Receive Your Free Mail Order Catalogue
and Quilting Bee Newsletter**

Name ___________________________________

Address_________________________________

City_____________________________________

State________ Zip___________ Country_____________

WC95